SPECIAL PEOPLE
SPECIAL PLANNING

Creating a Safe Legal Haven
for Families with Special Needs

PEGGY R. HOYT J.D., M.B.A.
CANDACE M. POLLOCK, J.D.

Foreword by Chad Nye, PhD
Executive Director, Center for Autism & Related Disabilities
University of Central Florida

Special People, Special Planning
How to Create a Safe Legal Haven for Families with Special Needs
ISBN 0-9719177-2-8
Copyright © 2003 by Peggy R. Hoyt and Candace M. Pollock

Published by Legacy Planning Partners
251 Plaza Drive, Suite B
Oviedo, Florida 32765
Phone (407) 977-8080
Facsimile (407) 977-8078

Printed in the United States of America.

DEDICATION

To our clients and colleagues who give meaning to what we do.
Thank you for your presence and your wisdom.

For more information or to order a copy of this book,
visit www.specialpeoplespecialplanning.com

Cover Design by Kimberly D'Angelo, Archer-Ellison/bookcovers.com
Interior Design by Julie Hoyt Dorman

Table of Contents

Forward

Special People, Special Planning may be one of the most important books you'll read. Some years ago as I was leaving a convention center at the conclusion of a conference focused on special needs individuals, I watched as an elderly mother and father and their 60+ year-old son moved toward a shuttle bus to go to the airport. I had been sitting in meetings for several days listening to speakers talk about the need for family estate planning for special needs children. I had been thinking about the difficulty a family experiences when they have to deal with both the daily living needs of the special needs person, and think about and plan for the long-term care of the special family member. I began to think about what would happen to this adult son when his parents were no longer alive to see that his life needs were met adequately? Who will be responsible? How much will it cost? Where will the resources come from? Will other family members or relatives be there to help?

As the Executive Director of a program that serves individuals with autism spectrum disorders and their families, I know how important estate planning can be for family members with special needs. The information in this book provides the reader with a basis for thinking about and planning for the future. It is a clear presentation of the fundamentals that every family needs to consider as they plan for their loved one's future. As most of us know, winding our way through the legal system can seem like a maze without an exit. Special People, Special Planning is a guide to understanding that maze and providing you with knowledge of available options that you and your legal advisor can use to plan for the support and caregiving you desire for your loved one. Each chapter will probably raise as many questions as it provides answers. That is a great benefit to us. *Special People, Special Planning* will makes us think and talk about important family matters; how we will support and care for each other, who will be responsible, how will the resources be appropriated, and a whole host of other issues.

We do not want the courts dictating what happens to our families when we are no longer able to voice our views. *Special People, Special Planning,* will at the very least help guide you in a decision making process that focuses on your values, beliefs, wishes, and choices. I commend this book to you and trust that the result will help you in creating the kind of future you and your special needs family member desire.

Chad Nye, PhD
Executive Director
Center for Autism & Related Disabilities
The University of Central Florida
Orlando, Florida

Preface

This book is intended to provide an overview—for the everyday person—of the many considerations and options that might be available to them when planning for the security of their special loved ones with a disability. It has been our experience in advising clients over the years that if they understand, in general terms, how a legal process works and where they might fall within that process, they tend to be better consumers and more confident about their choices.

Getting a handle on special-needs planning can be a difficult task—even for lawyers and financial planners who deal with complex terms and concepts for a living. There is no central source of information on the topic and, often, the information available can seem to be conflicting. Like the parable of the blind men describing an elephant, it seems that each resource approaches the topic only from its own perspective, which makes it difficult to see how the various components of special-needs planning interrelate.

To complicate matters, the rules and policies involved in planning for people with special needs call upon common law concepts, federal laws and agencies, and state laws and agencies, as well as local agency interpretation of state and federal rules. There are significant variations from state to state and even from county to county. Even for lawyers who are trained in research and complex legal concepts, it can be difficult to see the rules for the forest of exceptions to the rules. It is not uncommon to have a conflicting interplay of factors.

In this book, we attempt to point out how to create a good, sound foundation for planning for a loved one with special needs. The approach is basic to any good estate planning: Work with counseling-oriented attorneys and advisors within a team approach, become educated as to options and maintain a mechanism to keep the plan updated to stay current with changes within the family as well as the law.

Although the book necessarily involves a lot of complex concepts, we have attempted to eliminated legalese whenever possible. We include a glossary in the appendix with terms that are used during the planning process. The definitions are intended for the layperson and not for legal scholars. We do not cite case law and regulations, since this is not intended to be a legal treatise. We intend to provoke thoughts and questions that a person can consider as they enter the planning process about what they want and what they need to achieve for their special loved one.

We would like to gratefully acknowledge our many colleagues who have contributed their insights, wisdom and inspiration on this topic over the years. We are appreciative of them all as we certainly share a common bond—a genuine concern for people and their special needs loved ones. It would be impossible to properly credit them for the work, ideas and expressions of philosophy that we have woven into our practices from educational conferences, articles, legal chat rooms and phone calls. We have endeavored to determine whether previously published material included in this book required permission to reprint. Please accept our apologies if there has been any failure to provide proper credit or if there has been an error or omission of any kind. We will be happy to make corrections in subsequent editions.

CHAPTER 1:
The Need for Special Planning

I t is believed that today approximately 15 million families in the United States have family members with special needs. Statistics show that people with special needs are living longer and, in many cases, have normal life expectancies. They are more likely than ever before to outlive their parents and, perhaps, even their siblings.

Planning for special needs family members has always been necessary. However, with longer life expectancies and greater societal expectations about the quality of life that they can and should enjoy, planning is a necessity since parents and other family members might not be around to look after their special loved one. Without special planning, how are family members and future caregivers expected to provide for these special people? Where will the resources and services come from? How will anyone know the family's wishes, hopes, dreams and desires as well as their fears, frustrations and anxieties regarding their loved one? These are all part of creating special planning for special people.

There is no well-defined, well-accepted definition of special-needs planning. In some circles, "special-needs planning" refers to the requisites for maintaining the comfort and happiness of a special person when those extras are not being provided by a public or private agency. In other circles, "special-needs planning" can refer to the variety of programs and services required by a person with a disability, including medical and dental expenses, training, education, treatment and rehabilitation. Or it can refer to the "extras"—those additional goods and services that increase quality of life.

For our purposes, a "special person" is anyone who requires special consideration regarding their personal care and support due to cognitive and/or physical impairments —whether or not the impairments meet the definition of disability under federal or state social service programs. The special person could be a minor, an adult child, a sibling or a spouse. For convenience sake, in this book we will generally approach the topic from the perspective of a parent planning for a special needs child. However, be aware that the word sibling or spouse could be interchanged for parent in many situations. There may be times when a planning technique requires the participation of only a parent, sibling or grandparent and not a spouse. We will do our best to point out these requirements when necessary. A special person will include minors born with special needs or adults under the age of 65 with special needs (either from birth or adult onset).

"Special planning" is the creation of a financial and legal blueprint to address the special person's unique personal, financial and social needs. The plan can permit family members and loved ones to provide "extras" to protect the special person from becoming vulnerable to exploitation by others and to augment government financial assistance programs without disqualifying the special person from such programs.

During their lifetimes, families provide the emotional, financial and personal support for their special person. They act as their special person's advocate in the medical, legal or social program arenas. Society has evolved over the years to make public programs available for such families to provide educational, therapeutic and vocational opportunities for the special person. The families fill in the nooks and crannies between programs to ensure that their loved one gets what they need in light of their special person's specific physical and/or cognitive condition. Together, the families and programs can promote maximum independence and quality of life for the person with special needs.

Families must plan for the day when they are no longer available, due to their own disability or death, to fill this crucial role for their loved one. Although good, sound estate and financial planning is at the core of planning for a person with special needs, having a plan that is specifically tailored to the individual special person is essential. To ensure a personalized plan, the family must consider:

1) Their resources in terms of family, friends, advisors, case workers or therapists;

2) The family's personal financial resources, currently and in the future;

3) The public assistance programs for which their special person is currently eligible or likely to be eligible in the future.

As a rule, the standard of living and quality of life necessary to provide families with confidence in the future of their special person can't be met solely through public assistance programs. Nor are family resources likely to be sufficient. Therefore, special-needs planning should consider procedures to preserve lifetime public benefits for their special person while maximizing personal financial assets.

Traditional estate planning techniques provide poor outcomes for such situations. Traditional estate plans that leave funds outright to the disabled person can cause the person to become ineligible for government assistance programs or cause them to be vulnerable to the undue influence of others or give them direct access to funds they are ill prepared to deal with. Failure to provide funds for the disabled person can tax the resources of remaining family members or leave them at the mercy of others who are not equipped to take care of their needs.

There are many ways to fulfill a family's intent regarding how the family will provide for the special person after the original caregiver's own disability or death. However, not all legal and financial advisors are familiar with the special considerations associated with planning for individuals with disabilities. It is important to identify a team of advisors who can work together to craft a plan that will best meet the family's needs for their special person, within their personal and financial resources.

It is never too early to plan. Today is not too late; tomorrow might be. Death or the idea of it shouldn't be the only impetus to begin the planning process. Instead, the focus should be on planning for life and all of its uncertainties. Imagine taking a snapshot of your family and your plan as it exists today—this instant. What does it look like? What if you were unable to make any changes? What would you do differently if you could make a change? Your good intentions without action always have unexpected negative results. Have you considered all of the variables that can affect your family's plan? There are a number of noteworthy pressure points in a family's life that may encourage planning opportunities.

These would typically include:

1) The special person's 18th birthday;
2) The death or disability of a parent;
3) The loss of government entitlement programs due to improper planning.

People put off estate planning for many reasons. The reasons most often mentioned:

1) They don't know how to begin;
2) They don't know who to turn to for assistance;
3) They have concerns about costs;
4) The process seems too difficult and overwhelming.

Failure to craft your own plan means that the "default" plan provided by your state law will control. The state's plan rarely matches a family's desired plan under the best of circumstances, as outlined in later chapters. When families have to plan for the needs of a special person, the state's default plan will normally spell disaster. The chapters that follow will outline the planning process for creating an estate plan for you and your unique family circumstances.

CHAPTER 2:

Maximizing and Protecting Public & Private Resources

I t is generally well accepted that access to government benefits is essential to a special person's overall well-being. Family resources can be used to fill the gaps and increase the special person's independence, quality of life and dignity. Family resources can make the difference between a reasonable quality of life and one of mere subsistence. The majority of families with a special person pay a significant amount of out-of-pocket expenses that don't fall within public assistance and medical programs. Good coordination of public and private resources permits parents to provide a good quality of life during their own lifetimes and after their deaths.

There are three main federal disability programs. All require an applicant to show they meet a certain level of disability defined by the law. Some of the programs, such as Medicaid and Supplemental Security Income (SSI), also require an applicant to show financial need for benefits. Their assets or income cannot be above certain levels even if they meet the disability guidelines. These programs are called "needs-based" programs.

Some programs, such as Social Security Disability Insurance (SSDI) require the applicant to show, among other things, that they are disabled and had employment which contributed to the Social Security system for a specified number of quarters prior to the onset of disability. Some children are eligible for the program because their parents' employment history satisfies the earnings contributions for the required quarters. Some programs require contribution from the applicant on an "ability to pay" basis.

Prior to the age of majority, parents have a legal duty to care for and support their children whether or not the children have special needs. Consequently, parents' resources and income are attributed to their off-spring for purposes of needs-based public disability programs. In technical terminology, the process of attributing one person's income and resources to another is called "deeming." This means that for such programs a minor special needs child might meet the disability standards of a program but not the "needs" test because the parents' income and resources are deemed to the child.

However, in most states, when the child reaches the age of majority, the child is no longer automatically considered a dependent in the eyes of the law and the parents are no longer legally obligated to support their off-spring—even if their child is unable to be self-supporting. Therefore, the income and resources of the parents are no longer deemed to the child. Assuming the special person's disability impairs their ability to produce income and secure resources in their own name, the special person—at the age of majority—will meet both tests of disability and reduced-income resources for the "needs" test and be eligible to receive public benefits.

Public benefit programs may be authorized under federal law and administered by the individual states. Each state has leeway in how it administers the federal program. A state's administration is referred to as "state-specific" rules. For instance, some states, but not all, require that when a Medicaid recipient dies, the recipient's estate must reimburse the state for the benefits the recipient received. Therefore, familiarity with a specific state's application of a program's rules is essential in planning how to coordinate public and private resources for a special person.

Congress showed it does not intend for families to face an either—or dilemma of public versus private resources when it passed the Omnibus Reconciliation Act of 1993 (OBRA '93). Through OBRA '93, Congress created "safe harbors" under which families can provide private resources to their special people while maintaining eligibility for public benefits— as long as strict guidelines are followed.

The key phrase is "as long as strict guidelines are followed." The rules controlling these safe harbors or havens are complex and must be followed to the letter. After determining the special person's medical, financial and social needs, it is important to identify the programs to which the special person is likely to be eligible, now and in the future. Then it is crucial to understand which rules regarding resources and income apply to the programs in order to weigh the pros and cons of the various estate planning options that should be used.

Family members or friends who might make a gift to the special person or might be called upon to supervise the special person should be apprised of the overall estate plan to ensure the plan is not inadvertently sabotaged through a well-intentioned but unexpected bequest or gift. These family members and friends should be educated regarding the rules about coordinating public and private resources to prevent such an event.

In very simplistic terms, a plan can be constructed to stay within the safe haven rules authorized by Congress by not placing assets in the individual name or control of the special person. In this way, a "partnership" of public and private resources can be created to support the special person financially, medically and socially in ways that are not likely to be achieved solely by relying on one resource or the other. The pros and cons of various estate planning options follow this chapter and must be considered in the context of the individual cognitive and physical abilities of the special person as well as the overall goals and values of the family.

CHAPTER 3:
Guardianship

Parents do not retain the same legal authority on behalf of their child once the child has reached the age of majority, as that term is defined in their state. In most states the age of majority is age 18. In some states it is age 21. We call a person who has reached the age of majority an "emancipated adult." There are some circumstances when a child can be emancipated in the eyes of the law prior to the chronological age of 18 or 21, but for our purposes we will use the traditional 18 years as the age of emancipation. Once the child has been emancipated, someone, even the child's parents, must petition the courts to be appointed as legal guardian when the child lacks the capacity to make their own decisions.

A guardianship is a court-approved status granted to one person, the guardian, on behalf of another person, the ward. State probate laws set forth the standards of proof that must be met before the court will permit the guardian to act on the ward's behalf. Once the standards have been met, the status of guardian and ward will continue so long as there is no proof of a change of circumstances to warrant a revocation of the status. Therefore, in theory, a guardianship can remain in place for the ward's lifetime even if the actual person filling the role of guardian may be different over time.

The guardianship process (called a conservatorship in some jurisdictions) is also sometimes called a "living probate" because the rules controlling the process appear in the state's probate code. There are basically two categories of guardianship or conservatorship depending on the circumstances. Each type grants the guardian or conservator different powers. A person can be appointed as a "guardian of the person" and/or a "guardian of the property" depending on the needs of the ward. A guardian of the person will typically have physical custody of a ward and make day-to-day living decisions while a guardian of the property will be authorized to manage the assets and make financial decisions for the ward.

Being appointed guardian requires court involvement and, for so long as the guardianship remains in place, court supervision and periodic reports to the court are required to satisfy the court that the guardian is carrying out their duties appropriately. Consequently, there are attorneys' fees, court filing costs, costs associated with preparing financial reports for the court and, perhaps, costs associated with reports from medical or other professionals reporting on the status of the ward. And, as with any probate process, the entire process is public record.

A guardian will not be liable for the acts of the ward but will be held to certain standards of care in relation to the ward. The standards of care are set forth in Chapter 6, which addresses fiduciaries and fiduciary duties.

Although parents will be given preference as guardians, the court can appoint guardianship to someone else on behalf of the adult child if it feels the circumstances warrant it. The biological or adoptive parent is called a "natural guardian" and is normally given at least guardianship of the person. If the court feels the parents lack sophistication or are subject to undue influence or some other grounds exist to justify the decision, the court can give guardianship of the assets or estate of the ward to someone else while the biological parents retain guardianship of the person.

Parents should begin consulting with legal advisors regarding the guardianship procedures in their state prior to the special child's 18th birthday, if that is the age of majority in their state and the child lacks legal capacity. The legal advisor can tell the parents the type of evidence they will be required to present as well as the costs and time frames associated with the process in their community.

It is important to note that prudent parents will prepare estate planning documents that make arrangements for the care and support of minor children whether or not the children have special needs. The documents should name the parents' selection of guardians for the court to consider. This is called "nominating the guardian." The documents should name successor guardian candidates if the initial candidates are unable to serve. If the parents have particularly strong feelings about family members they do not want to serve as guardians of their children, it is appropriate to set this forth in the documents as well.

If the named guardian candidates are a married couple, it is recommended that the document identify the parents' wishes as to which partner of the couple should retain custody of the ward in the event of divorce. Again, although the court is not bound by any of the nominated candidates, the parents' nominations will give the court some guidance on the matter.

There are alternatives to guardianship. However, as presented in Chapter 4, it is generally recommended to have guardianship status established to add a measure of authority when acting on behalf of the special person who lacks legal/mental capacity to make decisions for themselves.

CHAPTER 4:
Planning Options

Just as disabilities can take many forms, the estate plan for a special person can take many forms. The exact nature of the plan will depend on the nature and severity of the special person's current and anticipated disability. Many special people can have physical disabilities and/or health impairments that do not affect their ability to manage their own personal or financial affairs. Some will never have the ability to make such decisions independently. Others have progressively deteriorating mental or physical conditions that create the risk they may lose their ability to manage their own personal or financial affairs at some point in the future. The special person's eligibility for public benefits can be independent of these planning considerations. The combinations of options and considerations make clear that boilerplate, off-the-shelf estate plans have no place when planning for a special person.

The concept of The Protection Spectrum (see Figure 1) can be used to distinguish the types of protections available for beneficiaries. You may ask, "Protection from what?" Generally, the protections that can be provided range from creditor protection to divorce protection to asset management protection to catastrophic illness protection. In simple terms, protection from both creditors and predators.

The correlation between the protections available to a special person and the degree assets are held or distributed to that person, or even to a non-special needs person, is graphically represented on the spectrum. There are little or no protections on the left end of the spectrum, which represents outright distribution of assets to the beneficiary. There is increased or maximum protection on the opposite end of the spectrum, where the assets are protected because distributions are made based on a limiting standard such as health, education and maintenance (HEM). The distribution can be as liberal or conservative as the trust creator desires. Varying degrees of protection exist in the middle, where distributions are staggered or made by some specified formula or standard. The degree assets are available or distributed can create or defeat protections against creditors or costs associated with catastrophic illness, divorce, and eligibility for needs-based public benefits, just to name a few.

(Figure 1) **The Protection Spectrum**

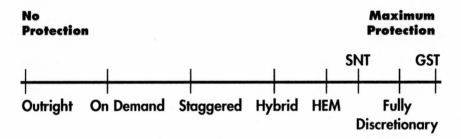

[Note: Although we are presenting this material in the context of planning for a special person, the correlation of protections and availability of funds is true when planning for any beneficiary. Long-term protections for any offspring-beneficiary can be included in an estate plan where the desire exists for protections against divorce, creditors, spending habits, etc.]

The traditional ways people might arrange their estates are set forth below. Keep the protection spectrum in mind when assessing these methods. We will present the methods from least protections for the beneficiary to most protections. For example, "Doing Nothing" would appear on the far left of the spectrum because it would, in most circumstances, result in outright and unfettered distribution of the parents' assets to the special person-beneficiary. Outright distribution of assets provides no protections to the recipient because whatever is available to the recipient is available to their creditors and predators. If a recipient has unrestricted access to funds, they will, therefore, be ineligible for public programs until those funds are exhausted.

On the far right hand side of the spectrum are "Trusts." A properly designed trust can accomplish many goals, from simple probate avoidance and mental disability protection to more sophisticated planning that contemplates estate tax avoidance or reduction strategies to special-needs planning and generation-skipping techniques.

Do Nothing—No Formal Planning in Place

State law controls what happens to someone when they are mentally disabled but there are no legal documents in place (e.g., durable powers of attorney and healthcare proxies) to direct how to carry on their personal affairs while they are unable to do so for themselves. This set of state laws is contained in the state's probate code under the guardianship and conservatorship rules. The process of applying these rules to an incapacitated person is sometimes called "living probate" because it requires the intervention of the probate court to make decisions about how to handle the person's affairs—while they are alive but mentally incapacitated.

These rules will guide the probate court regarding who has authority to make decisions for the incapacitated person when that person is unable to make decisions for themselves. Parents of a special person who fail to create legal documents in the event of the parents' incapacity can place the parents and the special person at the mercy of the state laws and court system. State laws might not create a plan that is consistent with how the parents want matters handled for their special child or themselves. Clearly, the special person and their parents have lost some measure of control over their destiny when no formal disability plans are made.

State laws also control who gets things held or titled in a person's individual name when there is no valid will to direct the court otherwise. This set of state laws is contained in the state's probate code under the "intestate succession" rules. "Intestate" means the person died without a valid will. "Succession" refers to the sequence or pecking order in which relatives of the deceased will receive the deceased person's individual property. For instance, under many state laws of "intestate succession," a surviving spouse will get a specified portion of the estate value along with the home during their lifetime and the children will get equal shares of the remaining estate value. Property held in joint title or with beneficiary or payable-on-death designations is not controlled by the rules of intestate succession.

Parents of a special person who die without a valid will or alternative planning in place can trigger the intestate succession or living probate laws. These laws can have many adverse effects for a special person—especially if the special person is currently receiving public assistance or likely to do so in the future. The special person will be at risk, personally and financially, while the lengthy living or death probate process transpired. No one will have clear legal authority to act on the special person's behalf until the court process was complete. There will be a risk that the special person might receive assets outright in their own name and control when they do not possess the maturity or skill to manage those assets and when the receipt of such assets will likely make them ineligible for public assistance benefits.

Doing nothing and making no formal plans for oneself never makes sense. Doing nothing and making no formal plans when a special person is involved is irresponsible.

Powers of Attorney

Powers of attorney are legal documents that identify who has legal authority to act on the power giver's behalf. There are various characteristics of powers of attorney, and some documents might be "powerful" under some circumstances and not others. Therefore, it is important to understand the differences among the various categories of powers to decide which ones are most likely to achieve one's desired goals.

The person who gives the power is called the principal, grantor or assignor. The person who is identified as the possessor of the assigned power is called the "agent," the "assignee" or the "power holder." Powers can be general or specific, durable or springing, or a combination of these. A power of attorney is not presumed to be durable or springing unless specifically identified as such.

Multiple powers of attorney can be given to any number of agents, although doing so is not recommended because the agents may take contrary actions on behalf of the grantor. Rather, it is recommended that the grantor either name two agents who will act together or identify a first agent and successor agent in the event the first agent cannot serve. Additionally, the grantor can name a mechanism by which a successor agent is selected if the first agent cannot serve.

Durable powers of attorney retain their powers when the grantor is mentally incompetent. Although it may seem counter-intuitive, if a power of attorney doesn't specifically state it is durable, it is powerless during a period of the grantor's incompetency. This means the power of attorney may not be effective at a time when it is most needed.

In some states, powers of attorney can be general or they can be specific and limited. General powers of attorney set forth a broad range of acts the agent can carry out for the grantor and often state that the agent may perform any act the grantor can carry out for themselves. Limited or "special" powers of attorney limit the scope of the agent's authority to itemized activities, a specific scope of activity or a specific period of time.

Powers of attorney can be "springing" powers, meaning the authority under the document is not triggered until an identified event occurs. For example, the springing power might contain language that says the agent's power is effective when the grantor is confined to a hospital, is out of the country or is incapacitated. Sometimes it can be difficult to know if and when the trigger event has occurred or there may be a difference of opinion as to whether the event has occurred. This may be especially true if incapacity of the grantor is the triggering event.

There are a number of disadvantages associated with powers of attorney. There is no court supervision of agents operating under powers of attorney. General powers of attorney can be the equivalent of a blank check, and the selection of an agent should be given careful consideration. Specific provisions can be incorporated into the document to create a panel of decision-makers, for instance in the case of sophisticated investment decisions. A court might have to become involved—after the fact—if a grantor discovers abuse and takes some court action for restitution. By that time, of course, it is generally too late.

Discord between family members can also be a drawback. If family members disagree with the appointment of the agent by the grantor or are suspect of the activities of a named agent, the unhappy party may begin a guardianship proceeding to have the grantor declared incapacitated by the probate court. The filing of the guardianship will, in most states, suspend the power of attorney and, therefore, the agent's power until the guardianship process has been completed.

Another disadvantage is third parties may be reluctant to rely on an agent's authority under a power of attorney. If this occurs, the agent can try to persuade the third party to accept the agent's authority under the document but, quite frankly, the agent does not have much recourse to force the third party to accept it. Some states have adopted statutes that impose damages, including attorneys' fees, if a third party unreasonably refuses to accept a validly executed power of attorney.

Reasons third parties might reject the power of attorney can range from the document being "too old" to springing clauses that are subject to differences of opinion as to whether they have been triggered. In the latter case and when the grantor is incapacitated, a living probate might be unavoidable if third parties won't rely on the power of attorney and there is no other way to accomplish the business at hand without the third party's acceptance of the power of attorney.

One way to reduce some of the risk that a third party might reject a power of attorney is to have the third party review the document before it is needed. The third party can advise the grantor as to whether the document needs specific clauses or clarification of current clauses to satisfy the third party's requirements. Although this is not a guarantee that future rejection will be eliminated, it can place the grantor in a better position to satisfy the third party's concerns when the grantor is not in a crisis condition.

Another problem associated with powers of attorney involves revocation of the agent's power. It can be difficult to notify third parties when a power has been revoked if the document has not been filed with a county recording agency. Powers of attorney can be filed with the local recorder's office for the purpose of making it part of the public record. In this way, third parties can review the public record to confirm the presence of the document. When a publicly filed power is revoked, the grantor merely files the revocation notice with the same agency and third parties will have notice of this as well. However, if actual notice of the revocation is required, there may be no reliable method to notify third parties of revocation of non-public powers or for third parties to know or be aware of revocations.

When a person is named as an agent under a power of attorney, they are given the power but not the legal duty to act in specified circumstances. It is important to understand that in some states, agents under a power of attorney may not be held to the same standard that a trustee would be held to under a trust document. More details will be given under the explanation of trusts and fiduciaries in Chapters 5 and 6.

Clearly, sole reliance on powers of attorneys to handle disability planning goals is misplaced. However, despite their inherent disadvantages, having a power of attorney in place is more desirable than having no such document in place. Proper counseling and drafting can dilute some of the disadvantages and can address some of the specific needs and goals of the grantor. Therefore, one-size-fits-all boilerplate power of attorney forms from attorneys who do not concentrate their practice in the special-needs area, do-it-yourself software packages or Internet sources are not recommended for a family that is planning for a special person.

Parents of a special person should have durable powers of attorney to take care of their own affairs and the matters pertaining to the needs of their special child—especially when the child is a minor. Similarly, at a minimum, the special child who has reached the age of majority and who retains competency should execute the appropriate powers of attorney authorizing their parents or others to handle their affairs in the event they are unable to do so for themselves.

Of course, if the special child is not legally competent when reaching the age of majority, the family will have to resort to the probate court for a living probate to have a guardianship and/or conservatorship created to establish the parents' authority to act on behalf of their special child.

Joint Ownership

There are several ways to jointly own an asset in most states. Joint tenants with rights of survivorship, tenancy by the entireties and tenants in common are examples of joint title in many states. Different types of joint ownership can trigger different consequences for a special person who is a joint owner with another—usually a parent, spouse or sibling.

Some joint owner titles contain specific survivorship provisions either by the very nature of the title (e.g., tenancy by the entireties) or by specific language contained in the title (e.g., joint tenants with rights of survivorship [JTWROS]). These types of joint title pass ownership to the remaining owner(s) upon the death of a joint owner(s) by operation of law. Assets that pass title by operation of law are not controlled by a person's will, and there is no need at death to go through the probate process to change title on that type of asset.

It is important for any family to understand the consequences associated with holding joint title to property since the operation of law can either support or defeat the disability and estate planning documents the family might have created. It is especially important for a family with a special person to understand the role joint title might play in their planning.

As an example, JTWROS property is subject to the claims of creditors of all joint owners. These creditors could be credit card companies, divorcing spouses, nursing homes or Medicaid. For instance, parents who intend to provide for a disabled child at the parents' death via the value in their home held in JTWROS might not own the property when the child needs it if the parents' creditors took it to satisfy debts. There is further elaboration of this risk under the section discussing testamentary trusts in this chapter.

In addition, property passing to the individual name of a special child would put the child at risk for the reasons set forth under Outright Gifts and as represented on the Protection Spectrum. Also, jointly held assets can raise issues associated with deeming the parents' assets to the special person who is a joint owner.

There can be income, estate and gift tax consequences when placing assets into joint ownership when the other joint owner(s) did not contribute value toward the acquisition of the asset. Some families will accept these consequences after assessing their options. However, most families are completely unaware of such consequences when opening an account with a special child. Certainly, few bank personnel are considering the entire family situation when they recommend a joint account as a convenient method to help manage the special person's affairs and to avoid probate.

Outright Gifts

This category includes gifts given during the life of and at the death of the gift-giver. The gifts can be received as cash or tangible assets; for instance, through a will or through unstructured payable-on-death or beneficiary designations on such things as insurance policies or retirement accounts. This category of gifts clearly exists on the far left of the Protection Spectrum, where they provide no protections for the special person. Since the gift will be under the full control of the special person, the gift will be fully available to their creditors and predators and will be, under most circumstances, a countable resource or income when determining their eligibility for needs-based public programs.

Outright gifts may or may not be an appropriate option depending on the likelihood of current or future availability or receipt of public benefits, the scope of such benefits or the capacity of the special person to manage assets that might be required to support them for a lifetime. As stated previously, failing to create a plan with some flexibility in the event that public benefits are not available or as extensive as currently known may subject the special person to hardship.

Disinheritance

Parents of minor children have a legal duty to support them. Parents of children who have reached the age of majority generally no longer have a legal obligation to support those children, whether or not the child has special needs and is unable to be self-supporting. Parents of special people can elect to effectively disinherit their special person—to preserve the child's entitlement to public benefits—by choosing to omit specific distributions to that child in their will or other estate planning documents. In these cases, the parents might leave a sentimental item of modest intrinsic value to the special person to demonstrate their love for the child. However, the item is not of sufficient monetary value to jeopardize the child's entitlement to needs based programs.

The disinheritance option often relies on gifts to other beneficiaries or siblings of the special person with the moral obligation that the recipient will provide for the special person during their lifetime. See Gifts to Third Parties below for more information on this option.

Divorce

When the special person is married, eligibility for needs-based programs can be precluded due to the deeming of one spouse's assets to the other—although this is an overly simplistic statement of the rule. Relying on the rationale for disinheriting a special person, divorce is sometimes seen as an option for married couples seeking to make the special-needs spouse eligible for needs-based programs.

Aside from the obvious social, religious, emotional and other legal ramifications of this option, there are some other disadvantages as well. Divorce is included in our list of options in the interest of being complete since we still occasionally hear of advisors recommending it as a solution. However, it is clearly an option of last resort and we recommend that a second opinion be obtained if other alternatives are not first offered as a solution.

Gifts to Third Parties on Behalf of the Special Person

As an alternative to disinheriting a special person outright—without other provisions—some parents might give the share that would otherwise go the special person to a sibling or trusted third party with the understanding that it is to be used for the benefit of the special person. The rationale behind this arrangement is that no assets will be directly available to the special person that might make them ineligible for needs-based public programs. The sibling will have legal ownership of the assets in the distributed share but, theoretically, will understand and agree that the assets will be used to provide for the special person the little extras that public programs can't provide. Such arrangements are sometimes called "moral gifts" because the sibling only has a moral obligation, not a legally enforceable obligation, to use the assets for the benefit of the special person.

In addition to the problems associated with disinheriting offspring, there are several other disadvantages to moral gifts: 1) The sibling has no legal duty to honor the moral obligation. The impact on the special person will be the same regardless of whether such failure was due to greed, misunderstanding or mismanagement or for reasons outside of the sibling's control; 2) The asset will be subject to the sibling-third party's creditors, such as through divorce, since it will be in the sibling's name; 3) There is no formal or legally enforceable mechanism for replacing the role of the sibling when they are no longer able to fill this role. The sibling's children might not know or agree to abide by the moral obligation; 4) The rules governing needs-based programs are complicated. The sibling might inadvertently purchase something for the special person that will trigger a period of ineligibility for needs-based programs. For example, if the sibling gives the special person money to purchase a gift for a friend, the special person's receipt of cash might make them ineligible for benefits.

Trusts

Trusts are contracts created by an individual (the trustmaker) that arrange to have assets held in the name of a designated person or entity (the trustee) for the benefit of another party (the beneficiary). Trusts can provide families with legal and practical mechanisms for addressing their own personal and financial needs as well as those of their special person. Trusts must be drafted in accordance with state laws. In the case of trusts for special people, the rules for federal assistance programs must also be considered.

The basic rules governing trusts require that there be 1) a creator of the trust, who is also known as the trustmaker, grantor or settlor; 2) trust property, which is also known as the trust corpus or principal; 3) a trustee in whose name the property title is held in trust; and 4) the beneficiary for whose benefit the trust is created. The trust document will identify these essential details and should contain many other details regarding the trustee's powers to manage the trust corpus as well as the circumstances under which certain powers come into play or are revoked.

There are many reasons to create a trust, and a person can have more than one type of trust depending on their goals, needs and resources. The standard reasons people create trusts include probate avoidance, estate tax avoidance, care of minor or special needs children and disability protection. Trusts will not automatically achieve these tasks. Many factors will determine whether a trust can accomplish its desired aim. For example, whether the trust is revocable or irrevocable, whether it is funded (discussed in Chapter 7) and whether the creator is also the trustee will dictate which tax or special-needs protections a person might achieve.

Careful drafting is essential with any trust. Careful counseling, drafting and administration of a trust for a special person can offer a family more options regarding the care and supervision of their special person and the management of the trust property. In very simplistic terms, the trust document clauses can serve as "babysitter instructions" for caring for the beneficiary when the original caregivers are unable to do so themselves due to disability or death. As with every other concept discussed here, standard clauses in boilerplate trust documents will produce poor results for special needs situations.

The following chapter will discuss the specific considerations required to draft a trust document that will reduce the likelihood that trust property held for the benefit of a special needs beneficiary will not cause the beneficiary to be ineligible for public benefits.

CHAPTER 5:
Trusts

There are different types of trusts, and there is a lot of legal jargon used in connection with trusts. Some of the jargon is interchangeable and some of it should only be used to refer to specific aspects of a trust. It is our experience that lay people are often intimidated by the jargon. However, if you keep the underlying principles in mind, after a while the distinctive uses of the jargon begin to make sense.

The first important distinction between types of trusts has to do with whether the provision for the trust appears in a person's will or in a trust document prepared during the person's lifetime. A provision for a trust appearing in someone's "last will and testament" is called a "testamentary" trust. A trust document created during someone's lifetime is called a "living trust." Living trusts can be revocable or irrevocable and can be "stand alone" or a sub-trust share of a parent's trust, depending on the terms in the document creating it. A person can have more than one type of trust to meet different needs. Prudent estate planners will prepare a variety of estate planning documents to address the spectrum of needs for the client. Therefore, a client's circumstances might require a revocable trust, durable powers of attorney, healthcare proxies, a pour-over will and a "stand-alone special-needs trust."

Testamentary Trusts

The testamentary trust is designed to come into effect at the death of the will-maker, called the testator. The details about the trust are set forth in the testator's will. The terms of the testamentary trust, just like the will itself, can be modified any time up to the point of incapacity or death of the maker.

Parents can design their wills to hold a portion of their assets at their death in trust for the benefit of the special person. In this way, no assets are ever received in the special person's own name to cause ineligibility for needs-based programs. No assets need be given to third parties with the unenforceable understanding that they are to be used for the special person's benefit. The trust can set forth the desired purpose of the assets, can arrange for family or professional management and can identify successor managers in the event that the original parties are no longer available to perform the necessary acts under the trust. Obviously, testamentary trusts have many advantages over disinheriting a special person and over moral gifts to third parties.

Despite these advantages, there are some disadvantages to testamentary trusts. Because a testamentary trust is part of a will, it must go through the probate process of the will. The probate process has inherent delays, costs and publicity. The special person might require the use of the assets before the probate process is complete.

The terms of the testamentary trust must be drafted and administered in such a way as to not make the special person ineligible for needs-based programs. Standard testamentary trust provisions will not produce a good result for a special person who needs to remain eligible for public assistance programs or who might be vulnerable to exploitation if funds are given to them outright or at staggered dates via standard trust terms. The drafting and administration considerations for trusts will be set forth more fully in the section regarding special-needs trusts.

Some additional disadvantages to testamentary trusts include the fact that there may be little or no trust property to place in trust for the special person at the time of the parents' deaths. At the time of drafting and executing the testamentary trust, the parents may have envisioned placing the value of their home or other assets into the trust for their special person. If these assets are not properly titled prior to death, they will not be available to fund the testamentary trust. In addition, in the years that ensue after executing the trust, the parents may have had to use those assets for their own needs, such as long-term care or support.

Because a testamentary trust does not exist until the death of the parent, it cannot receive lifetime gifts or death bequests from others on behalf of the special person. This means that others who might want to contribute property for the benefit of the special person will be required to either forego such gifts or create their own trust arrangement for the special person, keeping in mind the rules regarding public assistance programs. Obviously, this approach is inefficient and fraught with risk. This arrangement also does not contemplate inadvertent bequests when a special person might be the recipient of a bequest due to failure of others to adequately plan their estates.

Testamentary trusts have no mechanism to manage assets for the benefit of the special person during a period of a parent's mental disability since such trusts only come into play at the death of the parent and have no effect during the lifetime of the creator. Parents will need to be sure some other mechanism is in place to make sure their wishes are known and to implement those wishes when they cannot communicate them directly due to incapacity.

Living Trusts

A living trust is designed to exist prior to the death of the creator and is effective on the date of signature, assuming it is signed in accordance with applicable state requirements. Living trusts can be revocable or irrevocable. They can be stand-alone or exist as a sub-trust share of the creator's main trust. The decision about which option works best in a particular scenario requires an exploration of the family's situation, goals and resources. There is no automatic right or wrong answer. It is important to create a holistic plan regarding the family's goals to avoid "tunnel vision" planning by focusing only on one aspect of planning – especially when a special person's needs are involved.

The creator of a revocable living trust can modify it at any time prior to the death or mental incapacity of the creator. This means that if circumstances change within a family or if there are changes external to the family, such as market or tax law changes, the document can be modified accordingly if the creator is alive and competent. There are some exceptions to this rule, such as when a trust contains "trust protector" provisions, discussed in Chapter 6, which can permit some changes after the incapacity or death of the creator. However, regular updating while the creator is alive and well is recommended over reliance on trust protector provisions that might be subject to challenge.

Assets held in the name of a revocable trust are included in the creator's estate for taxation purposes and are available to the creator's creditors because the creator retains the right to add or remove trust property. The general rule is that anything to which the creator has access, the creator's creditors have access to as well. This gives the creator flexibility if they need the assets for their own use. However, it can place the assets earmarked for a special person at risk if the creator's creditors demand the assets to satisfy debts.

Irrevocable trusts generally cannot be changed without a court order after the trust is created. Property placed in an irrevocable trust is not available to the creator. Therefore, such property should not be available to the creator's creditors. This also means that property held in an irrevocable trust is not included in the creator's gross estate at death—with some exceptions. Irrevocable trusts can be designed to hold a specific asset item such as a life insurance policy. Such trusts are called irrevocable life insurance trusts or wealth replacement trusts.

It is possible to create more than one type of trust to accomplish different objectives. It is also important to understand the distinction between a sub-trust share of the parents' trust and a stand-alone trust to decide which type might work best in a particular situation.

A sub-trust share is created via a parent's living trust and generally sets forth conditions under which a portion of the trust property is earmarked for the benefit of a designated person. It operates similar to a testamentary trust in that the sub-trust share does not contain property of its own until the triggering event defined by the trust document occurs, generally the death of one or both of the parents. Using a word picture, the parent's trust is like a chest of drawers and the sub-trust is one of the drawers. A parent can create as many drawers, in different shapes and sizes, as needed to carry out their plan.

The stand-alone trust, on the other hand, is designed to exist separate and distinct from the parents' trust. It is like a separate set of instructions for a specific individual (or class of individuals) that exists regardless of the status of the parents or their trust. Lifetime gifts and property or testamentary gifts can be deposited into the trust account during the life of the beneficiary. Parents can assist in the management of the trust for the benefit of the beneficiary, and there is no probate delay as there would be with a testamentary trust. Family and friends may also make gifts to the trust for the special person without having to create their own stand-alone trust for the special person.

A stand-alone living trust for the benefit of the special person has several advantages: Assuming good market conditions and management, the assets can accumulate over a longer period of time with the potential for greater growth; the parents can observe the skills of siblings or other co-trustees to assess their skills and provide them with guidance; and family and friends will not need to make separate trust arrangements in order to leave assets for a minor or disabled family member.

Special-Needs Trusts

The term "special-needs trust" can be a term of art within the legal or financial planning communities or it can be a generic, descriptive phrase that refers to a trust with language that attempts to address the needs of a special person. A trust with language that merely attempts to address the needs of a special person does not ensure, however, that the trust will meet the rigorous guidelines set forth by the law to maintain a special person's eligibility for public benefits. Special-needs trusts are called by other terms as well, such as "luxury trust," "supplemental needs trust," "Medicaid trust," Medicaid Qualifying trust," "income trust" or "Miller trust." These terms are generally just a short-hand reference to a feature of the trust. For instance, a special-needs trust is designed to meet the supplemental needs of the special person, the luxuries or extras that are not met by the public benefits program; hence, the name "supplemental-needs trust." Sometimes the term is taken from the name of a particular court case that decided a rule of law pertaining to such a trust, such as a Miller trust.

As discussed in Chapter 2, the laws that govern whether someone receives public benefits are federal but are regulated by the individual states and administered by state agencies. Therefore, there can be tremendous variation from state to state regarding the specific types of trusts permitted, the terms used and the required language or provisions to stay within the state's regulations.

This is an area of law that is always evolving, and what was true 10 years ago may not be true today. In addition, the legal and financial planning community has some rules of thumb when it comes to which type of trust or what property should be placed in the trusts. However, it is best to be wary of any recommendations that are made without a thorough assessment of the family's situation and the current status of the law in your jurisdiction—especially when planning for a special person. The following discussion attempts to lay out the general requirements only. Obviously, state-specific rules governing trusts in general, state rules that control special-needs trusts and the specific needs, resources and goals of a family can cause the final trust document to vary significantly from family to family.

The term of art special-needs trust is a trust that is authorized by law and permits the trust to hold assets for the beneficiary to supplement the services provided by public assistance programs. The laws permitting such trusts are sometimes called "safe haven" or "safe harbor" laws because they permit the assets to be held safely for the beneficiary's use without making them ineligible for government assistance when the trust complies with the laws.

There are several categories of special-needs trusts that will normally all share the following features:

- The (disabled) beneficiary cannot be named as a trustee as is permitted in regular living trusts.
- The trustee has complete discretion to decide the type of assistance the trust should give, but in order to stay within the safe haven rules, the trustee should not exercise discretion to pay for services or items that are covered by the public program; the trustee should only expend assets to supplement, and not supplant, services or items provided by the government program.

- The trust should set forth a statement reflecting the creator's intent to create a trust that is designed to supplement and not supplant public assistance benefits.
- The trust should define what is meant by supplementary or special needs in both general and specific terms related to the unique needs of the special person.
- A description of who receives the remainder of the trust property if it is not all used during the lifetime of the beneficiary. Some of the sub-categories of special-needs trusts require certain "remainder" language.
- Certain "poison pill" language to set forth the disposition of the trust assets to alternate beneficiaries in the event the trust assets become subject to a claim for reimbursement for services.
- The trust should provide choices for alternate successor trustees when the initial trustee is no longer able or willing to serve in the role of trustee.

Third-Party Trusts

There are categories of special-needs trusts within the safe-haven rules depending on who created the trust and whose property is placed in the trust. Trusts are either created with the beneficiary's own assets (known as "first-party," "self-settled" or "payback" trusts) or by someone other than the beneficiary and with assets that did not belong to the beneficiary (known as "third-party trusts").

A third-party trust will always be created or established by someone other than the special person beneficiary and with assets in which the special person has no ownership interest. They are generally not governed or affected by OBRA '93. As a result, the creator of the trust has complete discretion to determine how the remaining assets will be distributed at the beneficiary's death. In addition, a third- party trust should not be subject to any claim by the state for reimbursement at the death of the special person beneficiary.

OBRA '93 Authorized Trusts

A trust created with assets that are deemed to or belong to the special person beneficiary must be established and administered according to the provisions of OBRA '93. There are basically three OBRA '93 trusts authorized under 42 U.S.C. Section 1396p: 1) "disability trusts"; 2) qualified income trusts; or 3) "pooled trusts." OBRA trusts are referred to as payback trusts because they may require the trust to pay back or reimburse the state for benefits provided to the special person beneficiary during their lifetime. In some instances, if assets are remaining after the state has been reimbursed, then family beneficiaries may be entitled to distributions.

Disability Trusts 42 U.S.C. Section 1396p (d)(4)(A). These trusts are also called "d4A trusts." To qualify for a disability trust the beneficiary must be under age 65 and must be disabled as defined by 42 U.S.C. section 1382 c(a)(3). The rules permit a parent, grandparent, legal guardian or a court to create and administer a trust for the sole benefit of a beneficiary. This trust is normally used when a beneficiary receives a distribution under an insurance settlement, a personal injury lawsuit or an inheritance that was not properly planned for. The outright receipt of such a distribution would make the beneficiary ineligible for public benefits without the use of the trust. Therefore, this federal statute creates a safe haven to permit specified family members of the beneficiary or a court to protect the award so it may be used to supplement the government benefits required by the beneficiary. Any assets remaining in the disability trust at the time of the beneficiary's death must be used to reimburse the state for money expended for the beneficiary's assistance.

Some debate exists as to whether disability trusts should carry very strict language that limits disbursements to supplement items only or discretionary language that will permit the trustee to selectively make distributions that may reduce government benefits, if needed. The trustee will be required to weigh the benefits of the supplemental services versus the reduction in benefits or the period of ineligibility that may be created for the beneficiary. The question that must be addressed by the family and the legal counselor designing the trust is: How much flexibility should the trustee be given in order to make value based decisions relating to the quality of life and services provided to your special person?

Qualified Income Trusts (QIT) 42 U.S.C., section 1396p (d)(4)(B). These are also sometimes called "d4B trusts," "income cap trusts," "Miller trusts" or "Utah gap trusts." A qualified income trust is most often used when the special person beneficiary requires long-term nursing home care. The qualified income trust can be created by a parent, spouse, grandparent, guardian, agent under a power of attorney, the court, or in some cases, by the beneficiary. A qualified income trust is designed to overcome the harsh result of disqualification from benefits when a special person beneficiary's income exceeds the required income limitations. Generally, the trust property consists of the beneficiary's income from pensions, Social Security or other sources. The portion of the income that exceeds the income limitation or cap is paid into the qualified income trust each month. The beneficiary is permitted a small personal allowance each month from the trust and the rest of the monthly income is paid from the trust to meet the beneficiary's portion of their medical bills. If any assets remain in trust at the beneficiary's death, the state is reimbursed for the services provided.

Not all states permit income trusts. Therefore, this type of trust, although authorized by federal statute, might not be available.

Pooled Trusts 42 U.S.C., section 1396p (d)(4)(C). A pooled trust is also called a "d4C trust," "master trust," or "community trust." They share the features of the disability trust rules that require the beneficiary to meet the definition of disability set forth in 42 U.S C. Section 1382 c(a)(3), and the trust must be created and administered for the sole benefit of the beneficiary. There is generally no age limitation to create a pooled trust. The trust can be created by the parent, grandparent or the legal guardian of the beneficiary or by a court. However, a unique feature of the pooled trust is that it also allows the special person beneficiary to establish a pooled trust on their own behalf.

These trusts are managed and administered by non-profit organizations for the purpose of pooling multiple trust property accounts for investment and management. A separate account record is maintained for each beneficiary, and the rules governing expenditures from the trust for the benefit of the beneficiary are controlled by the trust documents. The concept is similar to a mutual fund in which participants in the group can afford professional management and administration of the trust property without absorbing such management costs individually.

At the beneficiary's death, the federal rules control the disposition of any assets remaining in the beneficiary's individual account. The trustee of the pooled trust has the option: 1) to require assets to be used to reimburse the state for certain funds expended for the beneficiary; 2) to permit the pool to retain the assets for the benefit of others within the pool and the organization's overall purpose; or 3) to pass the assets to the beneficiary's heirs or others after the state's portion is reimbursed.

Pooled trusts can facilitate continuity and sophistication of management when the beneficiary's family and friends are few in number or not suitable for the task. Pooled trusts can also be a solution to situations in which the amount a family has to place in trust is too modest to be acceptable for most trust companies or banks or if the disability trust is not available due to the age of the beneficiary.

Some states have several pooled trusts available, while others have none, or the trusts have not existed for very long in that community. Pooled trusts can be vulnerable to failure for a number of reasons, but the primary reason offered is that: the average pooled trusts is originated under a community grant that is authorized to sustain it for a limited time period. Thereafter, the trust must attract other beneficiaries to join the pool to justify management and staffing costs. In light of the risk factors associated with some pooled trusts, it is important to assess it for viability to ensure that any assets placed with the pool can be retrieved for the beneficiary.

Other Considerations

A trust is only as good as the combination of the following factors: 1) comprehensive legal and financial planning or counseling to determine the best possible options for the particular situation at hand; 2) custom legal drafting for the best fit of the options to the individual's situation; 3) administration to ensure that any distributions from the trust stay within the applicable rules and are managed prudently; and 4) selection of appropriate individuals or entities to fill the various roles required to meet the needs of the beneficiary.

Factors that will enter into the counseling and drafting decision making are 1) a comprehensive legal and financial planning component with an assessment of the special person's lifestyle and day-to-day needs; 2) the degree of personal assistance, medical, social, employment and other active care requirements; 3) short-term and long-term financial needs and budgets, including identification of assets that currently exist or need to be acquired to fund the trust with projections of investment results and inflation; and 4) government benefits.

Obviously, if the family is attempting to structure matters for the care of their special person for the time the family is unable to provide it directly, they will want to give attention to the special person's social and emotional needs, too. Provisions can be included in the plan to facilitate social interaction and activities. For instance, language can be included in the trust to reflect the creator's intent that visits by family and friends are encouraged and funds are authorized for that purpose.

Regardless of the type of trust used, other matters should also be considered when drafting specific provisions of the trust:

1) Does the trust have provisions that anticipate circumstances that might develop and does the trustee understand basic concepts in order to ensure that they act consistently with the intent and provisions? The basic concepts might include the following:

   a. How will medical malpractice or negligence awards be handled?

   b. Can the trustees supplant public benefits with private services? And, under which conditions should this occur? For instance, although the program pays for medical care, can the trustee purchase some medical services privately?

   c. What guidelines should be followed regarding program restrictions on income?

   d. How do we deal with assets belonging to the beneficiary; e.g., an inheritance, gifts, accumulated income?

   e. Can other family members or friends contribute to the trust and retain control over the remainder interest attributable to their contribution?

f. How do increases in the cost of living (decrease in purchasing power of the dollar) affect administration of the trust?

2) Needs of others (alternate beneficiaries). Often it is necessary to fund a special-needs trust with more than what may be considered a fair share if the beneficiary did not have a disability. Generally, we want to treat our children equally. However, sometimes there is nothing more unfair than the equal treatment of unequals. In the case of a family that has a child requiring a resource for lifetime assistance, equality of treatment may be impossible. A trust is often established so as to give the ability to provide for the special person under the worst-case scenario. Therefore, given any scenario less than the worst case, the trust may be generating income beyond (and perhaps far beyond) what is necessary to meet the needs of the beneficiary. Under this circumstance, it is possible to include benefits to persons other than the special person. Some issues to consider include:

a. **Excess Income.** Defined as the growth in the value of the trust over the prior year's value that was not distributed for the special person or as required to be accumulated for an annual increase in the cost of living. If excess income is available, it might be applied to meet the needs of other individuals, such as other family members with disabilities or family members without disabilities.

b. **Borrowing.** Borrowing from the trust principal might be permitted by a designated group of individuals. Restrictions on borrowing might be limited to a percentage of the value of the trust at the time of borrowing, say 30 percent. In other words, the total all members of a designated group would be permitted to borrow might be no more than 30 percent of the value of the trust. Such borrowing could be on generous terms, such as reduced interest rates or flexible repayment schedules. The ability to borrow in this fashion could be a significant benefit if a need existed that could not be met out of excess income; e.g., college tuition, medical expenses.

c. **Expense reimbursement.** This should be clearly identified. It might include reimbursement for travel expenditures for family members or friends willing to interact with the beneficiary or serve in a fiduciary capacity so that their willingness to participate does not result in a financial burden.

d. **Donations or gifts.** The trustee may be legally limited in their ability to make donations or gifts unless this issue is specifically addressed and authorized. This could be especially important in situations when an expenditure benefits others, even tangentially, in addition to the trust's beneficiary. An example might be when a piece of exercise equipment is purchased for a group home where the beneficiary resides with the understanding that the other residents will use the equipment. The expenditure may be considered an abuse of the trustee's discretion unless the expense is specifically authorized. It is generally recommended that this type of authority be limited in amount and character.

e. **Remainder beneficiaries.** These are the named individuals or entities that share in the balance of the trust after the death of the lifetime special person beneficiary. These individuals can be other children or those people who were willing to provide continued care to the special person or they can even be charitable entities.

Special Letter of Instruction or Letter of Intent

The Social Security Administration thoroughly reviews the special-needs trust documents to confirm that they comply with the law. Regulations call for close scrutiny as to whether any trust assets or income can be deemed to the person with a disability or can be indirectly tied to that person. If the intent of the creator is not stated or is unclear to an interested agency such as Medicaid, the Social Security Administration or a court, the agency might inject its own idea of the intent. The risk with permitting the agency to interpret the creator's intent is that it might construe matters unfavorably to the beneficiary. Court intervention might be needed if there is a conflict between the creator's intent and the agency's interpretation of the intent. Of course, if the creator is deceased, establishing the creator's unexpressed intent is difficult at best.

If, however, the creator's intent is set forth, the agency would not need to inject its own interpretation. Statements of the creator's intent and purpose of the trust are recommended to avoid the need for court interpretation. The special letter of instruction or letter of intent also helps guide the trustee in interpreting the legalese of the trust regarding the creator's hopes, dreams and desires for the future of the special person. The special letter of instruction should provide all of the information future caregivers need to know in order to understand the needs of the special person. Details about their abilities, diet, medications, therapy, social activities and preferences should be included. Special letters of instruction and letters of intent are discussed in more detail in Chapter 11.

CHAPTER 6:

Fiduciaries, Attorneys and Other Scary People

Proper planning for a special person requires the application of many skills by the advisors involved in the creation and management of the plan. The advisors need to understand and respect the elements that support the overall well-being of the special person and their family in addition to technical expertise regarding the legal requirements, the financial planning components and the emotional and social impact of the plan.

The estate planning documents identify the people who are to act on behalf of and for the benefit of the special person. The estate planning documents also authorize those people to take or refrain from taking action and set forth their powers under the documents. Basic rules of law governing trusts and agency (when one person acts on another's behalf) and fiduciary responsibility give further information about what the agents can do for their ward or beneficiary.

There are many roles that must be filled while the plan is being counseled, designed, drafted and administered. Sometimes the same people can fill several roles. Other times it is advisable to have some roles filled by different people. This chapter is intended to provide an overview of the various roles that come into play in a special person's plan, the duties associated with those roles, and some ideas about how to select the best candidate for those roles.

The terms discussed are often intimidating—or scary—to people who don't use them regularly. Although people might sometimes use these terms interchangeably, in the eyes of the law each term is actually a "term of art." A term of art means the word carries a distinct legal meaning for practitioners of the art. For example, in the medical field, lay people might use the terms "sprain" and "strain" interchangeably. However, to a medical practitioner, the terms are similar but distinct with a technical difference between them. In our casual everyday language it is often unnecessary to worry about the distinctions. In the legal field, sometimes the distinction is very important indeed.

While we won't get into most of the nitty gritty details that make up the distinctions, we will attempt to identify why some terms are used in one context and other terms are used in another context. We will discuss some of the factors to keep in mind when deciding who will best serve in the various roles, and we will give some pointers about how to interview some of the professionals who act as advisors or fiduciaries. With this in mind, we will answer the following questions: What is a fiduciary? What is a trustee? What is a guardian? What is a conservator? What is an attorney? What do they all have to do with the special person?

What is a Fiduciary?

The term "fiduciary" can refer to a person or entity, and it can refer to a standard of care that person or entity is required to maintain in relation to another person or entity. More specifically, a fiduciary is a general term for a category of person(s) or entities that have been entrusted with the responsibility over another person or that person's assets or matters. It is a person or entity that acts for another for the benefit of that other person or entity. In the context of the special person, the fiduciary will care for and make decisions for the special person, manage their assets, administer funds and make distributions according to the written instructions, both during the lifetime of the special person beneficiary and thereafter.

When one has a "fiduciary responsibility," it means they have the obligation to give their utmost and complete loyalty to the beneficiary when handling matters for the beneficiary. Among other things, this specifically means a fiduciary is not permitted to self-deal or profit at the beneficiary's expense. State laws can specify other standards for the various categories of fiduciaries. Types of fiduciaries include trustees, guardians, conservators, personal representatives, executors or administrators of estates and attorneys.

What is a Trustee

As previously stated, a trust is a legal arrangement regulated by state law in which one party holds property for the benefit of another party. The party holding the property is called the trustee. The trustee is a fiduciary person or an entity selected to carry out the purpose of the trust for the benefit of the beneficiary of the trust. In other words, the person or entity has been "entrusted" with performing duties for the benefit of the beneficiary of the trust. The rules governing fiduciaries require the trustee to act with the highest standard of care regarding the beneficiary and trust property and within the explicitly stated powers of the trust. The trustee is also permitted to use implied powers that would be required to permit the trustee to carry out the purpose of the trust as long as the powers are not illegal and they are consistent with the laws of the state where the trust is administered.

Selecting a Trustee

The trustee for a special person must have complete familiarity with managing trust assets and the rules that govern special-needs distributions on behalf of the beneficiary. A perfectly drafted plan for a special person can trigger ineligibility for government benefits if an improper distribution or purchase of assets occurs. Therefore, it is important that a trustee, or a panel of trustees, be selected who can manage the financial affairs of the trust consistent with maintaining eligibility for government benefits while being sensitive to the emotional, spiritual and social needs of the person for whom the trust was created.

A trustee must be over 18 years of age or a bank, a financial planner, a certified public accountant (CPA), an attorney or a professional fiduciary, such as a trust company or advocacy organization. Parents generally act as the original trustees for their special person. The parent-trustees can work with others to provide or obtain professional financial guidance and legal advice. The parent-trustees can retain the power to replace advisors as needed.

It is important that the parent-trustees identify who will replace them at their death or disability or, at least, the process for replacing themselves as trustees. The parents can consider having someone they have identified as a successor trustee serve concurrently while the parents serve to permit the parents an opportunity to observe the successor's style of managing the trust and the special person's affairs. In this way, the parents can give guidance to the successor regarding their child or remove them from successor status if it becomes clear they do not have the required maturity and skill to look after the special person.

Although any trustee will be held to fiduciary standards, such standards cannot ensure personal attention and knowledge of the specific likes and dislikes of the special person. This is where other written instructions like a special letter of instruction become important. The parents can provide a special letter of instruction to act as a roadmap for any successor trustees regarding their special person and their unique personal circumstances.

It is common for people to act as trustee of their own revocable living trust in non-special-needs situations. However, this is not permitted for a special person—even if the special person has the mental capacity to do so. It is important the special person never be given the power to direct disbursements of trust principal or income. If the special person has the power to direct payments from the trust, the assets within the trust may be deemed to the special person which, in turn, will make them ineligible for government benefits.

Successor trustees can be other individuals, banks, professional trust companies or advocacy groups. It is important to carefully review the successor trustees' experience regarding public programs and supplemental or special-needs trusts. Some entities, such as banks or trust companies, often require a trust to have at least a specific dollar amount of assets before they will agree to become trustee. Sometimes the management fees are more than can be justified for smaller trusts.

Of course, such entities can be technically proficient and comply with fiduciary standards but not provide the kind of personal attention parents of a special person would hope for their child. There may not be ways to avoid this. However, it is better to identify the parameters for selecting such an entity than omit provisions in the event that all family members and friends can no longer serve.

Sometimes the best choice of trustee is a combination of both family and professionals. Each can bring their own unique set of skills and services to the role of protecting the special person.

What is a Guardian or a Conservator?

As discussed in Chapter 3, a guardian or a conservator is a fiduciary person or entity that has been selected to make decisions for the best interests of their ward. The ward can be a minor or an incapacitated adult. In making decisions for the best interests of their ward, the guardian will be responsible for decisions about housing, education, medical care, activities, travel and other personal aspects of the ward's life for the health and safety of the ward and their assets. The probate code outlines the guidelines guardians need to follow. Chapter 3 discusses the role of guardian and the guardianship process in more detail.

Generally, a guardian does not require a license or any special training. Some states, however, do impose an educational requirement in the form of a state-provided course for the purpose of providing the guardian with the educational and legal framework necessary to carry out their responsibilities. Any qualified individual over the age of 18 can serve as a guardian, but many individuals, known as professional guardians, have made it their life's work to provide guardianship services. A guardian may also be a professional organization that employs a number of individual guardians for the purpose of providing guardianship services.

What is an Executor or an Administrator?

An executor or administrator (and in some states, referred to as a personal representative) is a fiduciary who has been selected to probate and carry out the terms of a will or the distribution of a deceased person's assets if there is no will. If the person selected is female, they may be called an executrix or an administratrix. By definition, probate will be a court-supervised process and the standards to which the executor or administrator is held are outlined in the state's probate code.

What is a Trust Protector?

Drafting an estate plan requires the estate planner to make many judgments based on the facts, resources and laws existing at that time. Estate planners will also anticipate future needs under the plan and build in provisions that will offer some flexibility should the needs of the beneficiary, resources or laws change in the future. Unfortunately, the planner can only build in a limited amount of flexibility. Beyond that, the plan must be updated, and sometimes completely rewritten, to be sure it remains consistent with the needs of the beneficiary as well as the current laws and resources. If the plan is not updated, the beneficiary must live with the plan as written.

There are times when updating cannot be done by the original parties, either because they are mentally incapacitated or they have passed away. The remaining beneficiaries can then be left with a plan that is a poor fit for their needs—not the result the original plan creators had in mind. A remedy to this situation is called the "trust protector." The trust protector is a legal concept that has been around for a while but tended to be utilized only within a narrow scope of trusts. Current uncertainty regarding the estate tax laws has caused planners to rethink how they can use the trust protector in a broader range of trusts to help their clients maintain flexibility into the distant future, when it is likely the original creators of the trust are no longer around.

A trust protector is an agent named in the plan who is given the authority to make changes within the trust regarding some of the provisions. In other words, someone is named to fill the role of trust protector and is given the legal authority to make the kind of changes the original creators would have been able to make if they were competent or alive to do so. In addition, depending on drafting, the trust protector may or may not have fiduciary responsibilities and the attendant obligations imposed by such responsibility.

The scope of the protector's legal authority should be outlined by the original creators in the original document. The legal authority can include anything from changing institutional trustees to making changes within the document in order to maintain favorable estate taxation to withholding distribution of assets due to impairment of a beneficiary. Depending on the scope of authority, the protector may be called upon to make personal judgments regarding a beneficiary's emotional maturity or complex tax judgments. Obviously, then, the skills of the person selected must closely match the type of decisions they will be required to make. The breadth of the potential decisions points to the wisdom of appointing a committee of trust protectors, with majority rule or some other mechanism for decision making when there is a difference of opinion.

The original document can provide for reasonable compensation for the protector(s). There is some debate within the planning community as to whether and how to provide for the replacement of trust protector(s) when the original(s) cannot serve. Some planners recommend that the protector name a successor. Others point out it is better to set forth the specific mechanism for replacing protectors rather than relying on the protector to name a replacement, since the original protector might succumb to incapacity or death before they have named a successor.

In the context of trusts for special people, the inclusion of a trust protector in the plan can permit the parents to have greater confidence that the plan will remain as flexible as possible for the needs of their child. The protector can keep the plan fine-tuned to the latest changes in the law as well as the needs of the beneficiary.

There are a number of potential disadvantages of incorporating protectors in trust documents, however. Foremost is the potential for conflict among the beneficiary, trustee and protector. Although, in theory, the trustee and protector have the same objectives in mind, they might have differences of opinions as to how to achieve those objectives. If they cannot agree on a course of action, the trust can be tied up while they resolve their differences. Careful drafting can build in mechanisms for decision making and resolving differences of opinion.

What is an Attorney?

Attorneys are known by different names, such as lawyer, counselor or counsellor, solicitor or advocate. Some terms from old English times are esquire or barrister. These are all terms of art that have historical origins that, in most circumstances, have long since lost their importance. The distinctions are not important for the purposes of our discussion. These days, it seems that the terms attorneys might use to identify themselves are based more on personal preference rather than on a real legal distinction.

Each state has its own educational, licensing and professional requirements for attorneys who want to practice in that state. All states require attorneys to obtain extensive educational training in order to be prepared and able to represent a client. To qualify to practice law, most states require attorneys to earn a law degree—referred to as a Juris Doctor, or J.D.—and pass a state bar examination. Most states, but not all, also require the attorney to continue their education for the duration of their legal careers by requiring them to attend a minimum number of classes on legal topics each year.

Attorneys are subject to codes of ethical conduct and professional responsibility imposed by their state's Supreme Court which supervises the licensing of attorneys in the state. Grievances against attorneys are administrated by their state and/or regional bar associations. The legal bar associations are professional associations of attorneys and can exist on state, county and city levels, depending on the size of a legal community.

The profession, as a whole, monitors its members to make sure they adhere to the ethical and professional rules within the state.

Attorneys can be sole practitioners, members of small firms or members of large firms. An attorney can be an associate, "of counsel" or a partner. Attorneys can be general practitioners (sometimes referred to by other lawyers as "threshold lawyers"—they take anyone as a client who can cross the threshold!) or attorneys can concentrate in a particular area of the law.

In addition to the type of law attorneys may practice, they can be plaintiff oriented or defense oriented within that type of law. They might be trial attorneys, called litigators, which means they have a practice that focuses on trial work, or they can be "transactional" lawyers who concentrate on some of the non-litigation aspects of the law, such as corporate, real estate or estate planning. Then there are attorneys who refer to themselves as "relationship-oriented" attorneys because they prefer to have an on-going, mutually rewarding and beneficial relationship with the client over their lifetime rather than for a single transactional event.

Selecting an Estate Planning Attorney

Selecting an attorney will depend on many different factors—not the least of which is the purpose for which you are interviewing attorneys in the first place. It is important to think about attorneys in the same context as doctors: You wouldn't hire your family practitioner or gynecologist to conduct brain surgery despite the fact they have the same underlying educational foundation. Additional training and years of specialized practice in a particular area of the law are important factors in selecting the right professional for your legal needs.

Selecting the right attorney is critical. However, just seeking a competent attorney is often not enough. Consider the personal qualities your attorney should have before you start interviewing candidates. Things you should look for:

- Scrupulous honesty and integrity
- Sensitive and perceptive communication
- Good judgment and common sense
- Discipline and toughness
- Creativity in finding constructive solutions
- Bar affiliations, professional designations, advanced training, specialization

Board Certification or Specialist

Each state has different rules about whether and which categories of the law will permit a board certification or specialist designation. In fact, some states use the term "board certified" and other states use "specialist" to identify an attorney who has met the criteria for the designation. There was a time when board certification or specialty was limited to one or two areas of the law, such as admiralty or patent law. In recent years, more specialties and board certifications are being permitted in many states.

These designations are voluntary for attorneys. Board certification or specialty requirements vary from state to state and as to the type of law for which the attorney is seeking certification. Certification often requires additional continuing legal education requirements and may require the applicant to pass a certification examination. There may be additional requirements that the attorney practice in the area of specialty for a number of years, devote a required percentage of their practice to the specialty area, handle a variety of matters in the area to demonstrate experience and involvement, and/or obtain favorable evaluations by fellow lawyers and judges. It is only when the attorney has passed the test and meets the criteria that they may call themselves a specialist. For example, an attorney who has met the requirements for a specialty in patent law could publicly state this on their letterhead and firm correspondence. Generally, the specialty designation must be renewed periodically by reapplying for the designation and sitting for a current specialty test. The state's Supreme Court will normally maintain records as to whether the attorney's license includes a specialty designation.

Attorneys who have not met the requirements for specialty in a particular area of law, assuming the state permitted such specialty, would not be able to use the term of art, "specialist." When referring to their practice, however, they could use terms such as "focus" or "concentration" and similar terms.

Some attorneys might choose not to obtain a specialty designation even if it is available in their state. In any event, we recommend you seek out an attorney who concentrates their practice in the estate planning and special-needs planning arenas, as these are technically difficult areas of the law that require a high level of skill.

Effective special-needs planning requires a high degree of specialized knowledge and expertise. General practice attorneys or even general estate planning attorneys do not necessarily possess the knowledge or expertise to provide comprehensive special-needs planning services or the ability to keep pace with future law changes.

Selecting the right estate planning attorney for you means doing your homework—educating yourself, defining your needs, learning to value professional services and seeking guidance in the selection of a qualified individual. Proper estate planning, especially for a special person, revolves around your relationship with your estate planning attorney.

Unfortunately, there are many businesses that claim to offer estate planning services. Not all of them are attorneys. Sometimes they are attempting to sell wills, trusts and other estate planning documents without the involvement of attorneys in the counseling, design and drafting of the plan or documents. Their approach is based on a transaction mentality—once you've signed your newly created plan, you are done. There is no discussion of the need for ongoing counseling, updating, support and maintenance. Likewise, there is no information being provided regarding the costs of updating, maintaining and, ultimately, the administration of the estate of the person for whom the plan was created. This often leads to planning "tunnel vision." Options can be overlooked or can even contradict planning that is already in place.

The legal professional has spent thousands of dollars and years of time learning how to analyze problems and to distinguish the simple from the complex. Finding a simple solution to a complex problem has as much value as unraveling a complex situation that may appear simple. Professionals add value to their services by their knowledge, skill and wisdom, continuing education, independent perspective and willingness to take responsibility for the results.

Planning for a special person requires careful selection of all professionals associated with the plan. However, the attorney's contribution to the plan is the foundation for everything else that follows. Therefore, it is important to be sure the attorney has specific experience in special-needs planning. Although attorneys generally cannot reveal the names of clients, they can obtain permission from clients to be used as references.

The attorney should be fluent in all types of available government benefit programs and have methods for staying current with changes in the laws and the application of the laws at the state and local level.

The attorney should be willing to work as part of a team of advisors who will contribute their expertise to the special person's plan. The attorney should provide guidance or direct the family to sources for guidance on being a trustee and administering the trust for the special person.

Social service agencies and advocacy groups will generally have the names of attorneys with whom they have worked and with whose work standards they are familiar. There are directories of attorneys, such as the *Martindale Hubbell Law Directory,* that list attorneys by region and type of practice. However, many of these directories only permit a listing for a fee and some qualified attorneys may have chosen not to participate. Member organizations such as the National Academy of Elder Law Attorneys (NAELA) and the National Network of Estate Planning Attorneys (NNEPA) provide lists of attorney members, legal education programs and specialty certifications for their members. Their member lists are available to the public for the purpose of locating a qualified legal professional in your area.

Once you have selected several names, you should interview the attorneys to determine whether they potentially meet your needs. The following is a list of questions you can ask:

- What is your experience in this field?
- Have you handled matters like mine?
- What are the possible problems or concerns in situations like mine?
- How long do you expect this matter to take?
- How will you communicate with me?
- Will you be my only contact or will anyone else be working with you?
- Is there a charge for the initial consultation?
- Do you offer educational workshops on the subject?
- How do you handle your legal fees? Do you charge by the project? Do you charge a percentage? Do you charge by the hour? What is your hourly rate? How long do you expect this will take?
- Beyond fees, what types of expenses do you expect to incur?
- If I need to make changes, how will the fees be handled?

- When will I pay? How often will I receive a bill? If fees are not paid on time, will interest accrue?
- What alternative recommendations can you make?
- Will I sign a formal fee or engagement agreement?
- In the event of a dispute, do you recommend mediation, arbitration or litigation?

Legal fees and costs should be discussed in detail before you get your bill. Attorneys' fees can vary dramatically depending on the nature and scope of the legal services provided. The scope of representation is an understanding as to what the attorney will do (or not do), how long it will take, what the attorney will not do without further authorization, what the client's goals are, and so forth. Financial arrangements should be as clear as possible. The maxim is to "put it in writing" to avoid misunderstandings. Many state bar associations recommend and even require written contracts for legal services.

Some attorneys provide services on a flat-fee or quoted-fee basis while others charge by the hour or on a contingency basis. The hourly rate usually incorporates one rate for attorney time and other rates for staff and law clerk times. Some state bar associations have ethical guidelines as to whether a case can be handled on a contingency basis or retainer or hourly. Some local court rules give guidance about the usual and customary range of fees attorneys can charge for such things as probate services. It is important to clarify whether a retainer (like a down payment toward services to be performed) is required and whether a fixed amount is expected each month as services are performed.

It is also important to understand the types and estimated costs that are likely to be incurred with the legal services. Some firms charge extra for legal research fees, paralegal costs, long distance phone charges and facsimile and copy charges. It is important to discuss whether you will be notified prior to the attorney incurring a cost—especially if the cost is more than a specified amount.

Hourly fees generally coincide with a lawyer's experience and/or their geographic location. For example, an attorney in Los Angeles, Chicago, New York City or Washington, DC, is likely to charge a higher hourly rate than a comparable attorney in a smaller city. Likewise, the size of the firm may dictate higher hourly rates for both partners and associates than a smaller firm in the same location. Other factors that play into higher fees are the cost of rent, salaries for support staff and firm perks or benefits.

Fees may be negotiable, although, as a rule, not after the services have been provided. If you intend to negotiate with the attorney for the value of the services provided, it would be best to initiate that conversation prior to the onset of the representation.

The contract for professional services should set forth the mechanism for termination of the relationship and, in the event of a dispute between you and your attorney, how the dispute will be resolved. Further, be certain to understand how long the attorney intends to maintain your file and whether the attorney has processes or procedures for keeping you updated on changes in the law regarding services previously provided. Most attorney-client relationships are "transactional," which means the legal relationship for representation purposes is terminated when the scope of the transaction is completed.

Good legal assistance and advice is not a one-way street. You have to cooperate with your attorney if you genuinely want them to help you. The attorney-client relationship is privileged and confidential, so you need to take your attorney into your confidence. Here are some important tips:

1) Don't withhold information from your attorney. In the field of estate planning, it is critical your attorney know everything about

you and your loved ones, including all of your hopes, dreams, fears, aspirations, eccentricities and peccadilloes. Your attorney needs to know what it is like to be you or a member of your family. What does life look like for your loved ones if you are disabled or if you pass away? What assets do you own, how do you own them and who are the named beneficiaries? What type of planning have you done in the past? Without all of this information, the attorney will be unable to assess your situation and to educate you about the law and how it affects you, your family and your special person in order to achieve a result that will be in your best interest.

2) Don't expect simple or immediate answers to complicated questions. Attorneys are justifiably cautious in drawing conclusions or answering complex legal questions without consideration of all the relevant facts. An attorney knows there can be a number of answers to the same question and the law is rarely an open and shut case. Attorneys have also been trained to closely examine both sides of an argument and to think through the ways something could go wrong. You may find that attorneys frequently use lawyer words like "it depends," "possibly," "could be" and "there is a great likelihood." Rarely will attorneys use statements such as "guaranteed," "always" and "never." There are frequently a large number of factors that can cause any situation to have an unintended or unexpected outcome.

3) Keep your attorney advised of all new developments. In order to do a good job, your attorney needs to be apprised of facts that may have changed in your personal or financial situation. When the attorney has all the facts, they can use this information to provide you with relevant information regarding changes in the law or the attorney's experience.

4) Never hesitate to ask your lawyer about anything you believe is relevant to your situation. Your attorney cannot read your mind. Also, remember that attorneys are not psychiatrists, doctors, case managers, marriage counselors or financial advisors. You will still need a team of trusted advisors to provide you with answers to all of your relevant questions and concerns.

5) Follow your attorney's advice. You asked for it, you paid good money for it. Don't work against your attorney. If you attempt to second guess the attorney's advice by bouncing it off of friends and family, understand that the friends and family will not have the depth of knowledge of the law – and possibly even of your situation—upon which to draw proper conclusions.

6) Be patient. Don't expect instant results. Trust your attorney to follow through and follow up but don't hesitate to ask for periodic progress reports. You have a right to know exactly what your attorney is doing for you. If you've engaged the services of an estate planning attorney who practices utilizing a formal estate planning process, you should always know what to expect next.

Your attorney's primary duty is loyalty to you. Their fiduciary duty requires this. Their interest is protecting your rights and providing you with the highest possible quality of service. Early consultation with an attorney can save you trouble, time and money because:

- The solution to your legal situation may be easily resolved or prevented entirely, depending on the nature of your problem.
- The earlier you seek competent advice, the less time is generally needed to complete the work required.
- Information is generally more readily available when prompt action is taken. Within the estate planning realm, this may be especially

important in the event a person becomes mentally disabled or cata-strophically ill or dies before they have completed their planning.

- Many legal matters or strategies are time sensitive or may have a "statute of limitations." Failure to act in a timely manner may prevent you from acting at all.

Other factors to consider:

- **Your comfort level with the attorney.** Do they speak in terms and use language you can understand? Do they take the time to explain those questions that are still unclear to you? Do you feel rushed? Is the attorney taking the time to fully answer all questions regarding your situation? Has the attorney explained the retainer or fee agreement? Do you feel pressured to sign the retainer and run out of the office?

- **The attorney's work load.** A common misperception is that an attorney with a cluttered desk is unorganized and has too much work to do an adequate job. Ask the attorney how many clients they are currently handling. Are they feeling overwhelmed by their work load or outside commitments? What other projects are they working on? What are their outside interests?

- **Past results.** Past results are never a guarantee of future success, but knowing an attorney's track record or experience in your type of situation can provide added comfort if they have had continuing success in cases similar in nature to yours.

- **Malpractice insurance.** Some states and some state bar ethics rules require that an attorney include information in their retainer agreements as to whether they carry malpractice insurance. Some states merely require that the attorney notify a potential client if they do not carry malpractice insurance. Malpractice insurance is designed to protect you from the negligence of your attorney. If information concerning the malpractice insurance carried by your attorney is not included in your written retainer agreement, ask that it be included. If an attorney does not carry malpractice insurance, you may pay lower fees; however, if a material mistake is made on your case which affects the case's outcome, you may have legal recourse but no ability to recover financial damages from the attorney's personal resources.

- **Imagination.** This means the ability to imagine ways in which something might go wrong. It is always better to have a mechanism for addressing a potential problem in an estate plan than to have no mechanism.

- **Skill.** Skill includes familiarity with the law, with a technical field or with legal procedures, and with interpersonal communication. Although different attorneys have different skills and skill levels, Any attorney is legally permitted to handle any legal matter, so long as: 1) there is no conflict of interest; 2) the attorney can handle the matter competently (generally a matter of opinion—the attorney's); and 3) all other laws and rules of professional conduct are followed. Like other skilled professionals, attorneys develop skills in specific areas of practice. An attorney who is very skilled at matters of type X may need to climb a steep learning curve to properly handle a matter of type Y. Beware of general practitioners or those who have a threshold practice because these individuals, although they may be very good at some legal matters, may not have the specific expertise you need or require. Many attorneys, regardless of their practice area, feel competent to draft a simple will. Our experience has been and continues to be that there is no such thing as a "simple" estate plan, especially when there are issues involving a special person.

- **Intuition or good instincts.** Intuition may arise from previous encounters with a judge, an opposing attorney or some other decision maker in the matter at hand. Intuition can give an attorney a sense of how a decision maker is likely to react to various arguments being considered by the attorney. There may be no way to determine whether someone has good intuition, except to rely on your own intuition.
- **Good character.** Reputation in the legal community can be an indicator of character. References will provide some guidance on the level of esteem with which the attorney is held in the community.

Other factors that will also be important include, the resources available to the attorney, the time frame in which the attorney can attend to your matter, and so on. However, ultimately you must be comfortable with your attorney, because your attorney cannot help you unless you communicate with each other. Choose someone you respect, not someone who intimidates you or uses jargon when it isn't needed. Your calls should be answered promptly and professionally. You should not feel as if conversations with your attorney are being either rushed or dragged out. If you are not comfortable, let your attorney know. If the relationship doesn't improve, look elsewhere.

Don't assume you can't afford a lawyer. Investigate the matter with competent legal counsel first. In many instances, the cost of competent legal advice now can save you hundreds, if not thousands, of dollars later. If you still feel you can't afford legal help, you may want to consult with your local legal aid society.

Selecting a Financial Advisor

The process for selecting a financial advisor is similar to selecting an attorney. The financial advisor should be familiar with calculating the costs associated with the needs of a special person. Although the nature of the special person's disability will dictate some of the calculations, the financial advisor who has worked with families with a special person should be able to help the family determine the financial methods most likely to take care of two generations of family—the parents and the special person.

A financial advisor should read the family's special letter of instruction or intent for the special person and attempt to create a financial plan that will best meet their intent. Basic concepts of sound financial planning are essential in this process and, therefore, it is important the financial advisor create a holistic plan to avoid planning tunnel vision.

The financial advising community has various designations to reflect the education, background or orientation of the advisors. Some advisors may have a background in insurance, others in investment analysis, and yet others in general planning concepts. Although there is debate among planners as to whether a particular certificate or designation is required to be a good planner, the general view is that a planner who has acquired a particular certificate or designation within their field has demonstrated a commitment to the field by acquiring the designation. Interview potential financial advisors with the same goals in mind when interviewing attorneys. You have to be comfortable that your advisor is sensitive to your needs and goals, and has the qualifications necessary to create a financial plan consistent with those needs and goals.

The Importance of the Team Approach

It should be obvious that the legal advisor and the financial advisors should coordinate their advice to eliminate the possibility of invalidating the other's actions. For instance, if the family creates a trust for the benefit of a special person with the intent to supplement but not supplant benefits received through a public program, it would not make sense for a financial advisor to propose an annuity payable directly to the special person. Although this may seem unlikely, similar actions have occurred with unintended consequences due to failure of the advisors to work as a team.

In the real world, it is not common for advisors from different disciplines to consult with and coordinate their recommendations. This failure to coordinate might stem from ignorance of the other advisor's field, difficulty coordinating schedules or even arrogance. When dealing with a plan for a special person, it is imperative that the family seek out advisors who embrace the team approach to planning.

Coordinating the Team

Although some advisors will readily understand the importance of coordinated efforts when planning for a special person, such orientation in planning has not been the traditional method for many. The family might have to take the lead in asking that the advisors meet and coordinate their activities. The family can select an initial advisor and express their desire to have all team advisors participate with them in the planning process. Thereafter, a series of meetings of all advisors can be called to permit them to organize the required data, share their recommendations and, finally, to report on the completion of the plan stages. Often, advisors who use the team approach to planning can make recommendations of advisors in other disciplines they have successfully worked with to be part of the team and the process.

Other Possible Team Members

Depending on the special person's circumstances and the family's desires, it might be advisable to include input from clergy or medical advisors. This is obviously a matter of personal choice. However, if someone in the clergy or the medical community is a trusted friend of the family, the family might ask that they be included on the team for ideas on meeting the special person's needs.

The plan for a special person will require detailed record keeping and reporting, particularly if the special person is interested in maintaining eligibility for public assistance. Therefore, the services of a Certified Public Accountant (CPA) or other record keeper is important to the administration of the plan. Including such a person on the team of advisors and making specific provisions within the trust for them can lay a strong foundation for the plan. Later record keepers can follow the lead of the initial advisors to maintain the creator's intent under the plan.

Accounting-Record Keeping

Maintaining reports and other records for scrutiny by public agencies is essential to the viability of the special person's continued eligibility for benefits and for making sure the trustee has not deviated from the proscribed duties. Although lay people can perform some of the tasks and might do so without compensation, the plan should authorize payment for performing or hiring professional advisors, such as a CPA, to perform these functions. The financial planner's analysis for the special person should include a budget for the costs of professional advisors.

It should now be clear that the counseling, design, administration, funding and maintenance of a plan for a special person requires the time and coordination of a number of qualified individuals. A commitment to understanding the role of each of these important team members will ensure the ultimate success of the plan.

CHAPTER 7:
Funding/Asset Integration

A ny trust that has no money or assets earmarked for its use is worthless. Steps must be undertaken to make certain the trust is funded with assets designed to meet the intent of the creator as well as the needs of the beneficiaries, especially when those beneficiaries are people with special needs. "Funding," a term of art, means that the ownership of assets is changed into the name of the trust or the trust is the named the primary beneficiary of life insurance, retirement plans or annuities.

Funding the Special-Needs Trust

The creation of the documents for a special-needs trust is only the first step in the process. There must be sufficient assets, properly owned, in order to make sure there is sufficient money to last the lifetime of the special person.

It is at this stage of the planning process that the team concept of professional advisors becomes most critical. The attorney can create the legal framework; it is now up to you, in concert with your professional team, including a CPA and financial advisor, to construct a financial plan consistent with the goals and resources that will best suit the unique needs of your family.

Like attorneys, there are few financial advisors who have experience planning for the future of a person with special needs. The average financial planner is trained to look at the overall estate and try to provide as many dollars as possible while at the same time keeping an eye out for potential problems. If uninformed, the financial advisor's approach may be to try and provide as many dollars as possible for the special person without realizing the impact this approach may have on the individual's ability to remain qualified for their governmental benefits.

A financial advisor skilled in planning for families with special needs individuals will review your special letter of instruction and budget calculations in order to prepare a detailed financial analysis based on the projected future costs of supplementary items and needs as well as advocacy. The financial advisor will look at all the family's many different resources available to fund the trust both now and in the future.

There are often more resources than a family realizes that can be used to fund a trust; for example, existing government benefits, savings (now and over time), gifts from other family members, inheritances, future assistance from family members or friends, the family home, investments, and life insurance or retirement accounts directed to the trust. Getting the assets into the trust – the funding of the trust—requires either a change of ownership of the asset during your lifetime or naming the trust as beneficiary at the death of the owner.

The financial advisor should help the family make sure it has not overlooked sources of assets such as veteran's military benefits with survivor options. Insurance has been described as a perfect mechanism for families to either create wealth or to cover the cost of taxes on wealth. Insurance can be a method to leverage smaller premium amounts in order to leave a large lump sum for the future benefit of the special person.

The specific amount required to adequately fund the trust for the future needs of the special person is personal to each family and requires a detailed financial plan with projections about inflation, asset allocation and returns on investments. Some brokerage firms have been developing a niche in planning for the special needs community and may even be able to provide financial "calculators" designed for the unique needs of the family planning for a person with special needs.

A special-needs trust can hold almost any kind of asset or can be the recipient of any kind of asset that is payable on the death of the asset owner. Although some trusts, such as testamentary trusts, hold title to no assets until the death of the creator, it is generally recommended that stand alone trusts hold at least a minimum amount be placed in the trust to fund it initially.

Assets can generally be added to a trust over time. However, some special-needs trusts do not permit additions after the age of 65. Additions may be made by gifts during life, by a will or living trust, by life insurance policies, by employee plan benefits or by other retirement plan benefits.

CHAPTER 8:
Taxation

There are four categories of tax rules that can come into play with special-needs trusts: income tax (including capital gains tax), gift tax, estate tax and generation-skipping tax. The type of trust (self-settled or third-party) will determine the nature of the taxes incurred in the first three instances. The tax rules will determine who is responsible for filing tax returns and paying the tax.

Third Party Trusts

Third-party trusts must almost always meet the tax rules requirements to be a separate taxpayer with its own employer identification number (EIN) and obligation to file yearly state and federal fiduciary income tax returns.

Third-party trusts can be "complex" or "simple," although most will be complex trusts since by the terms of the trust the income is not to be paid to the beneficiary. These are terms of art under tax law. Under a simple trust, all income is taxable to the beneficiary whether or not it is distributed to the beneficiary. Under a complex trust, income is only taxable to the beneficiary to the extent it is actually distributed to them or for their benefit. A K-1 form is issued under the beneficiary's Social Security number each year setting forth the actual total income distributed to the beneficiary. The information obtained from the K-1 is then reported on the individual's annual income tax return.

Self-Settled Trusts

Self-settled trusts are generally "grantor" trusts for income tax purposes. Therefore, the income from the trust is attributed to the creator, known as the grantor, of the trust whether or not income was actually distributed to them. In other words, the income from the trust assets is "passed through" the trust to the grantor, as is the income tax. A separate EIN or taxpayer identification number is not generally necessary since the grantor's Social Security number is the number used on the reporting form for Internal Revenue Service (IRS) purposes.

Different rules may apply if the trust corpus comes from personal injury proceeds. The general rule is that personal injury awards are not subject to income tax except for the portion of the award that represents pain and suffering, punitive damages, interest or anything that is for non-physical damages. However, income generated by the investment of the funds will trigger income tax to the trust grantor.

There can be instances when the trust itself is responsible for the income tax. In this case the tax will be part of the trust administration expenses that can be deducted from the gross income without a 2% floor required on personal income tax returns.

Drafting will determine whether a trust is a grantor trust. There are drafting methods to achieve this: 1) give the beneficiary a special power of appointment; 2) give the beneficiary the power to substitute property of equal value; and 3) give the beneficiary the power to borrow from the trust without giving security for the loan. The beneficiary does not need to have the mental capacity to exercise the special power of appointment in order for that clause to trigger grantor trust status for income tax purposes.

Income for income tax purposes will not always disqualify a beneficiary under public programs rules on "in kind distributions." Therefore, it will be important for the representative payee to submit an explanation of the income for income tax purposes versus the public program's purposes. In other words, although the beneficiary of the trust will be charged with income for income tax purposes, they never were in actual receipt of the same for the public program's purposes. Therefore, the impact of the income will not disqualify the beneficiary for income-based qualification programs.

Estate Taxes

At death, a decedent's gross estate will include any property owned by the decedent, over which the decedent retained control, or property on which the decedent's name appears. When the beneficiary of the trust dies, the estate tax treatment of the amount remaining in the trust will depend on whether it is made up of guaranteed payments or any assets in which the beneficiary retained a beneficial interest. The IRS has provisions that determine how to value guaranteed payments. Basically, these provisions require a calculation of the present value of the future payments with a discount at a specified interest rate.

Normally, the balance of a self-settled trust will be taxed as part of the beneficiary's estate even if the trust was not subject to grantor trust rules for income tax purposes. Third-party trusts, on the other hand, will generally not be included in the beneficiary's estate for estate tax purposes.

If the trust corpus contains highly appreciated assets, the remainder beneficiaries may want to take advantage of the step-up in basis rules. Basis is the amount paid for an asset used to determine whether a capital gain will be due at the time the asset is sold. In this case, it is better for the assets to be included in the deceased beneficiary's estate in order to qualify for the step-up to fair market value treatment of the asset's basis.

To get this result, it will be necessary to have a clause that permits the beneficiary to exercise a general power of appointment. However, this type of power can have some major disadvantages, such as making the trust assets subject to the beneficiary's creditors or a claim by Medicaid. Therefore, the relative pros and cons of including assets in the beneficiary's estate are an important counseling issue.

Gift Taxes

Gift taxes are triggered on the transfer of property by gift—in other words, a transfer for less than fair market value. In the context of a special-needs trust, the question as to whether gift taxes are triggered turns on whether the third party, or the beneficiary with a self-settled trust, made a completed gift—defined as a transfer that gives up control over the property with no power to change.

There are several arguments that support the position that a gift has not been made for gift tax purposes in such situations: If property was transferred to a self-settled trust as part of a lawsuit settlement, no gift was made to the beneficiary-grantor since they are the sole beneficiary and the property was given as consideration in exchange for the release of claims against the defendant.

Gifts by individuals to a third-party trust can have gift tax consequences to the gift-giver (donor) if the value of the gift exceeds the annual gift tax exclusion amount, currently $11,000 per year. If a gift in excess of the annual gift tax exclusion amount is made in any one year, IRS Form 709, a gift tax return is required to be filed. The effect of the return is to report the excess gift to the IRS. Generally, there is no tax that must be paid, but the excess gift does reduce the donor's future ability to leave assets at the time of their death estate tax free. Gifts and their resulting tax implications should be coordinated with the certified public account who makes up the special planning team.

Generation-Skipping Transfer Taxes (GSTT)

The rules governing generation-skipping transfers can be important in the context of planning for special persons since the needs of multiple generations are often involved. A generation-skipping transfer (GST) is any transfer of property to another who is at least two generations younger than the giver. The transfer could be a lifetime gift, a gift at death (otherwise known as a bequest), a taxable distribution or a taxable termination. There can be GST implications where the remainder interest of a trust pass to a "skip person(s)." As mentioned earlier, a gift is a transfer of something for less than fair market value. A bequest is a gift made at death. A taxable distribution is a distribution of trust income or principal to a skip person who is not otherwise subject to estate or gift taxes. A taxable termination is a termination of an interest in property through death, lapse of time, release or waiver of a power, or other mechanism that causes the property to transfer to the control of a skip person—unless estate or gift taxes are imposed on the non-skip person at termination.

A grandparent who gives property to a grandchild will have made a generation-skipping transfer assuming the parent of the grandchild is still alive. If that parent is deceased, then IRS rules provide there is no skip of a generation. Similar rules apply to nieces or other collateral relatives if no living lineal descendant stands between them and the gift-giver. The IRS has specific rules for determining generations when the parties are not related.

Special rules apply if a trust is the recipient of the gift. Specifically, a trust may be considered a skip person if all beneficiaries of the trust are skip persons or if distributions from the trust could be made to non-skip persons. Otherwise, the beneficiaries of the trust would be assigned generations for generation-skipping transfer tax (GSTT) purposes.

Everyone has a cumulative lifetime GSTT exemption and an annual exclusion similar to gift tax exemptions and exclusions. The GSTT rate is the maximum gift and estate tax rate at the time the skip is made. Gifts that are tax free under the Internal Revenue Code do not trigger the GSTT. For instance, payments for another's education or medical expenses, gifts under the annual gift exclusion, and transfers previously subject to GSTT when the recipient was in the same or lower generation as the present recipient are not included for GSTT purposes.

The GSTT exemption can be allocated to specific gifts made during the donor's lifetime, and there is a great deal of sophisticated tax planning that can be done regarding the allocation in order to maximize a gift's effectiveness. The nature of the transfer determines whether the transfer is tax inclusive or exclusive. The allocation of the exemption can be wasted if consideration of the tax inclusiveness or exclusiveness is not made.

When skipping a generation is being contemplated, the planner should calculate the GSST as well as the gift and estate taxes that would be due if the transfer were made to the first generation (no skip). This requires sophisticated understanding of tax laws, which means the parties should consult with a seasoned pro in this area of taxation. Also, community-property states trigger rules unique to them. Therefore, if community property is involved, a practitioner familiar with community-property rules should be consulted.

CHAPTER 9:

Updating, Education and Maintenance

E state planning, including special planning for special people, may be viewed by some as a single transaction, something you get done and then don't have to worry about anymore. In addition, the initial planning process may have been emotionally traumatic for the family and it isn't an experience they want to have to repeat. You may be surprised to learn, then, that all estate planning requires ongoing updating, maintenance and family education. Creating the plan is simply the first step in a lifetime process.

There are a number of factors that can influence an estate plan over time:

1) Changes in your family or financial circumstances;

2) Changes in the law, both state and federal, that may affect the long-term operation of your plan;

3) Changes in your attorney's experience.

Changes in Your Family or Financial Circumstances

The first type of change an estate plan faces is change that directly affects you and your family, both personal and financial. Problems associated with this type of change arise as a result of your role as expert on yourself and your family. There is no way for your attorney and other planning professionals to learn about these changes unless you tell them.

Our experience has been that most people don't communicate regularly with their professional advisors, thereby putting their estate plan in danger of failing, or at least not meeting the family's needs as well as it might have prior to the changes. Sometimes, people are discouraged from communicating with their professional advisors because of the actual or perceived cost of communicating changed circumstances. In other words, people tend to communicate with their advisors less when they know there is an invoice attached.

Changes in the Law

The second type of change an estate plan faces is change to either state or federal laws, including the tax laws, changes to program benefits, limitations and restrictions, or laws that can affect the personal planning protections provided in your estate plan. Laws today change very rapidly, and only advisors who are actively engaged in special planning may be aware of all of the changes in the federal rules and at their local level and the impact on your special planning circumstances.

Changes in Your Advisor's Experience

The third type of change an estate plan faces is change in your attorney's or professional advisor's experience. Many professionals are committed to constantly improving their practices, their knowledge and the quality of their planning. Others continue to practice the same way they always have. Does your attorney have years of cumulative experience or are they still doing things the same old way? In Chapter 6: Fiduciaries, Attorneys and Other Scary People, look for guidance on evaluating your advisors' commitment to excellence.

An Estate Planning Solution—
The Three Step Strategy™

It's not about documents – it's about results! The key to proper estate planning is clear, comprehensive and customized instructions for your own care and that of your loved ones. These instructions can be included in your will, in a trust and in several other related documents. Regardless of the type of planning chosen, most people are best served with an estate planning process that revolves around a Three Step Strategy. The Three Step Strategy is an approach to planning that recognizes certain processes have to be firmly in place to create estate plans that work!

The Three Steps

Step 1) *Work with a counseling-oriented attorney (as opposed to a word processing-oriented attorney).* Much of what passes for estate planning in this country today is little more than word processing. We don't believe you should pay a licensed professional to fill out forms or to do only word processing. The value of a professional is in their counsel and advice, based on knowledge, wisdom and experience. If word processing is all you want, you might be tempted to do it yourself. *Be forewarned:* Theoretically, a person could self-diagnose and self-treat an illness or follow the medical advice given to another person with a seemingly "similar" condition — but is is not recommended for the safest outcome. If you want a plan that works, seek good counseling.

Step 2) *Establish and maintain a formal updating, maintenance and education program.* An estate plan faces a myriad of changes. First, there is constant change in your personal, family and financial situation. Second, there are inevitable changes in both federal and state laws that impact your estate plan. Third, there is (or should be) ongoing change in your attorney's and other advisor's experience and expertise. Your professional advisors should be continually improving their performance and expanding their knowledge through ongoing education and collective experience. Since everything, except human nature, constantly changes, you cannot expect a plan to accomplish what it was intended to accomplish if it is never updated. The costs of failing to update your plan are typically far greater than the costs of keeping your plan current.

The National Network of Estate Planning Attorneys informally polled their clients and discovered that, on average, people update their estate plans every 19.6 years! Has anything changed in the last 20 years that may have affected your estate plan? The last 10 years? The last five years? How about in the last year? Estate plans that don't work when expected result in a loss of benefits for loved ones, can result in litigation and worse, may cause family turmoil that undermines the structure of the family.

If your attorney doesn't offer a formal updating, maintenance and education program, discipline yourself to review your plan on a systematic basis. As you prepare to have your annual tax return prepared, this is a good time to get out your estate planning documents and review them with your professional team. Financial advisors generally offer or require annual reviews with their clients. This gives you a good opportunity to review the performance of your financial portfolio and to discuss and measure whether your investment strategy is still consistent with your long-term goals.

Your family assets should be reviewed on a regular basis to make certain that distributions made during life or upon death will not cause the disqualification of your special person from government benefits. Assets held in custodial accounts or as tenants in common, joint tenants with rights of survivorship (JTWROS), Uniform Gift to Minors Accounts

(UGMA) or Uniform Transfer to Minors Accounts (UTMA) may need to be shifted, re-titled or re-configured to preserve government benefit eligibility. Special care should be taken to review and change, if necessary, the primary and contingent beneficiary designations on all group term insurance plans provided by employers or professional groups, individually owned life insurance policies, 401(k) accounts, tax sheltered annuities and retirement plans like IRAs and SEPs. An individual with special needs should never be named as the outright beneficiary. Instead, the special-needs trust created for the benefit of your special person should be the proper beneficiary.

Meet with your attorney on a regular basis, not to exceed two years, to review your personal estate plan as well as the plan created for your special person. Include key family members, especially those individuals selected to serve as personal representatives, executors or trustees, in these meetings so they can begin the education process and understand the legal issues they may face in the future. Families that take the time to develop a long-term relationship with their legal advisors, to learn and understand the legal concepts that affect their family and who have a commitment to making sure their plan stays updated and maintained, have fewer problems when a family crisis arises and estate plans need to be implemented.

Step 3) *Assure fully disclosed and controlled settlement costs after your death.* The cost of any estate plan has three distinct parts: 1) the part you pay for counseling and design up front (or for word processing)—the cost today; 2) the part you pay for updating (or the potentially larger cost of failing to update)—the cost over time; and 3) the part your loved ones pay after death—the ultimate costs of settlement, administration and distribution. Regardless of the plan you choose (will-based, trust-based or other), there are always after-death costs. Wills are administered through a probate process; trusts have to be settled or administered. In either case, assets must be transferred to their intended beneficiaries and, often, final or estate tax returns must be prepared. Be sure you discuss and understand all three parts of the cost of your estate plan with your attorney before you begin to plan. Understand what all the costs will be in advance, and ask how they can be controlled.

The Importance of the Team Approach

As noted previously, creating an estate plan is not difficult, but it does require a commitment on your part as well as the involvement of all your professional advisors: your attorney, your accountant, your financial and insurance advisors, and your case managers and advocacy organizations. Depending on your plan, it may also require the participation of a planned giving professional for the charitable organization(s) of your choice. If all the professionals are included in the planning, you are far more likely to have an estate plan that works. If not, you may receive conflicting advice that leads to confusion and inaction. You may have heard the term "analysis paralysis" to describe the confusion and inaction that results when there are too many choices. The most effective approach is to involve all your advisors in your planning, and keep them apprised of steps you are taking. That way, everyone is fully informed and has a chance to offer their particular expertise to the process. A proper estate plan meets your goals and keeps you in control of the process and the results!

CHAPTER 10:
Termination

E ven the best plans can't predict all circumstances personal to the special person and their family or the external changes in the law or application of the law. Sometimes market conditions cause a serious drop in asset value or medical advancements help minimize a person's disability. Policy changes within an agency or legislature might also cause a shift in who will be eligible for benefits or what benefits are available to recipients. When circumstances change that cause the underlying need for the special person's plan to change, sometimes terminating the plan is appropriate.

Terminating the plan will trigger various consequences, depending on the nature of the plan, to whom the assets are paid at termination, and many other factors. Normally, a court order will be required to terminate the plan. The public agency responsible for the special person's benefits will also be an interested party in the termination process due to concerns about reimbursement of funds expended for the special person.

The court will be required, under the basic rules of law governing trusts and fiduciaries, to consider the rights of remainder beneficiaries as well as the rights of the special person. Depending on the court's ruling, income, gift or estate taxes might be triggered when the assets are released to the parties. Therefore, it is advisable to obtain the input of the same type of advisors who put the plan together regarding the termination of the trust.

In some states, it is advisable to include a "poison pill" provision that triggers termination of the trust if the trust comes under attack by a government agency providing benefits to a special person. The poison pill will provide the terms under which the termination of the trust is triggered and will identify to whom the remainder of the trust assets should be paid. The clause is intended to keep the assets free of claims by the government agency by transferring the trust assets to alternate beneficiaries. The intent could be that these alternate beneficiaries will then have a moral obligation to provide for the supplemental needs of the special person. As previously mentioned, a moral obligation is not a legal obligation, but in this instance may be the best remaining option for the long-term care of the special person.

CHAPTER 11:
Special Letters of Instruction

Ohe of the best ways to leave information for the care of your special person is a special letter of instruction or letter of intent. This letter may also be referred to as a future care plan. The special letter of instruction should provide all of the information future caregivers will need to know in order to understand your special person. Details about their abilities, diet, medications, therapy, social activities, mannerisms, and so forth should be included. If your special person requires assistance with the activities of daily living such as bathing, dressing, eating and communicating, you might also consider a family video showing and explaining how best to assist your special person.

Key Issues

The key issues to address in your special letter of instruction for the future of your special person are as follows:

1) **Lifestyle**—the day-to-day-assistance, medical, social, employment and other active care requirements of your special person;

2) **Legal planning**—including the location of wills, special-needs trusts, powers of attorney, health care directives, and living wills. Also critical are the identification and contact information for

guardians, personal representatives and trustees;

3) **Financial needs**—including the calculation of the special person's monthly budgetary needs and how much is required to fund the special-needs trust to provide lifetime resources for care. Identifying assets to fund the trust and projecting the effects of investment results and inflation should also be included in your special letter of instruction.

4) **Government benefits**—identifying the various Social Security and medical benefits including SSI, SSA, SSDI, Medicare, Medicaid and military pensions or other benefit programs your special person may be entitled to receive.

Families need to develop a clear vision of their hopes, dreams, fears, aspirations and goals they want for their special person after they are gone. The special letter of instruction should communicate that vision.

The letter should help the reader fully understand the nature of your child's diagnosis, prognosis, functional skill level, earning potential and abilities. A clear and definitive diagnosis is a basic starting point. This diagnosis can help lead to an accurate and realistic assessment of your child's functional skill level and future prognosis. A realistic prognosis can be developed to help lay the foundation for parental expectations.

The letter should be written to assist future caregivers. The letter can serve as a blueprint to provide valuable information in the daily life of your special person in the event a new caregiver has to step in and manage your child's day-to-day activities. In addition to vital information regarding your child's physical and mental status, the letter should include your child's likes, dislikes, hobbies, recreational and social preferences, food allergies, medications, physicians and medical history, as well as your hopes, dreams, fears, wishes and aspirations for the future.

The letter should also detail your thoughts on a variety of matters, such as dating, religion, sex, marriage, future living plans, and academic and job-readiness skills. The letter is not a legal document, but can function as a daily blueprint for future caregivers.

The letter, or multiple letters, can be written by parents, guardians, grandparents or other family members who describe the special person's history, their current status, and what you hope for them in the future. We advise you to write this letter today and add to it as the years go by, updating it when information about your special person changes. It is always easy to procrastinate when your health is good, the future looks bright and there are a hundred other pressing tasks to be done. However, no one can predict the future. September 11, 2001, taught us all that small probability events do happen. They can happen to you and to your family. What will happen to your special person if something happens to you? Will your relatives, friends, lawyer or the police know where to contact your special person? Will that person have enough information about your special person to know what kind of care is needed and how best to provide it?

When possible, it is also a good idea to involve your special person in the writing of this letter so that it accurately reflects the needs, concerns and goals of the special person. The extent to which you involve your special person will depend upon your special person's age and the nature and severity of their disability. If your special person can participate in the letter, it is also appropriate to involve them in the creation of the estate plan for their lives.

It is important to write a special letter of instruction, as it can serve many purposes. First, it can describe in plain English, your special person's background and history and their present situation. It can also describe the wishes, hopes, fears and desires you have for your special person and for their future care, along with your feelings about your needs and desires for your special person. The letter can be used by your attorney and other team members to draft the proper legal documents and create a financial plan to ensure your wishes are carried out.

When you are no longer able to care for your special person, due to death, illness or incapacity, the letter gives your special person's future caregivers some insight into how to care for your special person. The letter can provide advice on alternatives for care. If your special person has a severe lifetime disability, caregivers will not have to waste any time learning first-hand the best behavior or medical management techniques to use. If your special person can do things independently, the letter can describe exactly what kind of assistance is necessary. In addition, the letter can provide concrete information, including valuable information about the personality of your special person, their likes, dislikes, talents, special problems and strengths. The letter is a crucial part of any life or estate plan because it speaks both for and about the special person and their family.

Writing the letter is a way to protect your special person from unnecessary chaos and turmoil when they must depend upon someone else for the care and support that is necessary. Preparing the letter can be an emotional experience for parents and their special person. You will need self-discipline and motivation to work past many painful questions and issues that must be addressed when faced with an uncertain future.

The procedures for developing the letter can be fairly simple. You can write the letter in longhand, or you can use a computer or a typewriter. Don't worry if the spelling and grammar aren't perfect; your major concerns should be conveying important information about your special person to anyone who reads the letter in the future. Can they understand what you mean and what you would like to have happen? Begin any way you feel comfortable. We have provided a format for you to use as a guideline in Appendix C.

Once your letter is written, the most important thing you can do is let people know that it exists, what it contains and where it is located. You may want to tell your family members, relatives, neighbors, friends, clergy or spiritual advisors, or case manager. Tell them why you wrote the letter, what type of information it contains and where it can be found. The letter should be kept in an easily accessible place (not a safe deposit box at the bank) and it should be clearly identified. You may want to consider making copies of the letter to give to other children, family members or friends.

Like your estate plan, your letter should be updated on a regular basis. Choose a special day for reviewing and updating your letter each year—your birthday, your special person's birthday, December 31st, April 15th—whatever has meaning for you so you will remember. Talk with your special person and other family members each time you review the letter so you can add any new or important information. Update your letter every time something important changes, such as a change in circumstances, case workers, medication, and so forth. Each time you review and revise your letter, sign it and date it.

CHAPTER 12:
Conclusion

This book was written for the family and friends of special people. We have endeavored to help you and your family create an understanding of the issues related to planning for your special person in order to assist in the creation of a financial and legal blueprint for the future of your special person. It is our hope that your plan will be designed to promote family harmony, reduce burden and sacrifice, maximize all available resources and maintain quality and dignity of life.

We embarked on this journey for both personal and professional reasons. From a personal standpoint, both of us have been touched by family members who are special people; from mental retardation to the effects of premature birth and chronic illness. Professionally, we work in an environment in which we are exposed on a daily basis to the care and concern families have for the special needs of their special family members. Our goal is to help shed some light on this complex but absolutely essential (and often overlooked) area of planning.

There seems to be quite a bit of information on special-needs planning available in a piece-meal format. We were unable to locate everything we felt was important for a special family to know and understand in a medium that was both easy to obtain and easy to understand. We hope *Special People, Special Planning* comes closer to accomplishing this goal.

We are blessed by the resources available to us through the National Academy of Elder Law Attorneys (NAELA) and the National Network of Estate Planning Attorneys (NNEPA). These are organizations that provide us with the ability to interact with estate planning professionals dedicated to the best interests of their clients, to a never-ending array of educational workshops and continuing education opportunities, and venues to share our legal expertise through teaching and learning environments.

Thank you for joining us as we explored many of the difficult issues families with special people face. If you would like to be added to our mailing list so we can share changes in the law and in our experience that may affect your future and the future of your special person, please send us your email or mailing address at **www.hoytbryan.com, www.HAHN-POLLOCK.com** or **www.specialpeoplespecialplanning.com.** We invite you to communicate with us if there is anything we can do to assist you in the discovery, education and implementation process of creating an estate plan that works for you and for your special person.

APPENDIX A
Special People, Special Planning
Glossary Of Estate Planning Terms

Administrator— Person named by the court to represent a probate estate when there is no will or the will did not name an administrator. Also called an executor or personal representative. Female is administratix.

Ancillary Administration— An additional probate in another state. Typically required when you own real estate or assets in another state titled in your individual name and not titled in the name of your trust.

Basis— The amount paid for an asset to determine whether a capital gain will be due at the time of sale.

Beneficiary— The individual named in a will or a trust that is intended to receive the benefit of the assets.

Conservator— See Guardian.

Co-Trustees— Two or more individuals or entities who have been named to act together in managing a trust's assets.

Corporate Trustee— An institution, like a bank or trust company, that specializes in managing and administering trust assets. Can act as sole trustee or as a co-trustee.

(d)(4)(A) Special-Needs Trust a/k/a Disability Trust — Assets established in trust under 42 U.S.C. 1396p (d)(4)(A) using the disabled individual's assets. One of the OBRA 1993 payback trusts. Must be established by a parent, grandparent, guardian or the court. Beneficiary must be under the age of 65 and disabled. This trust is not considered a countable asset toward governmental benefit resource limits, but must contain payback provisions to government agencies after the death of the disabled individual.

(d)(4)(B) Special-Needs Trust a/k/a Qualified Income Trust— Assets established in trust under 42 U.S.C. 1396p (d)(4)(B) using the disabled individual's assets. One of the OBRA 1993 payback trusts. Must be established by a parent, grandparent, guardian or the court. Designed to overcome the harsh result of disqualification when the beneficiary's income exceeds government imposed income limitations. Any assets remaining in the trust at the beneficiary's death must be used to reimburse the state for government benefits.

(d)(4)(C) Special-Needs Trust a/k/a Pooled Trust— Assets established in trust under 42 U.S.C. 1396p (d)(4)(C) using the disabled individual's assets. One of the OBRA 1993 payback trusts. May be established by a parent, grandparent, guardian, the court or even the beneficiary. Trust assets are pooled for investment and management purposes. Must be established and administered by a nonprofit organization. Assets remaining at the beneficiary's death may be retained by the nonprofit organization or used to reimburse the State for government benefits.

Decedent— A person who has died.

Disclaim— To refuse to accept a gift or inheritance so it can go to the next named beneficiary. May be useful for estate tax purposes.

Durable Power of Attorney for Financial Matters— A legal document that gives another person full or limited legal authority to sign your name and act on your behalf in your absence. Valid through incapacity. Ends at death, revocation, termination or adjudication of incapacity.

Durable Power of Attorney for Health Care— A legal document that gives someone you name authority to make health care decisions for you in the event you are unable to make them for yourself. Also called health care proxy or medical power of attorney.

Executor— Sometimes referred to as an administrator or personal representative. The individual selected in a will to administer the estate assets. Female is executrix.

Fiduciary— Person with the legal duty to act for another person's benefit. Implies great confidence and trust, and a high degree of good faith. Usually associated with a trustee, personal representative or agent under a power of attorney.

Funding— The process of transferring your assets to a trust so the trust can control the administration and disposition of the assets. May include renaming the title to an asset or designating the trust as a beneficiary on life insurance, annuities or retirement plans. Also called asset integration.

Grantor— The individual who creates a trust. Also called a creator, trustor, settlor, or trustmaker.

Guardian— An adult individual named by a court and granted the legal power to make decisions for another individual (the ward) who is incapable of making their own decisions. A guardian could be a guardian of the person or a guardian of the property. A natural guardian is generally a parent. A guardian ad litem is generally appointed for a limited purpose to protect the interests of minor children or a person incapable of making their own decisions.

Guardian Ad Litem— A person, not necessarily a lawyer, who is appointed by a court to represent and protect the interests of a child or an incapacitated adult during a lawsuit.

Guardianship— A court ordered proceeding whereby the ward is declared incapable of managing their own personal and/or financial affairs. A guardian, either of the person or the property or both, is then named to manage the personal and property affairs of the ward.

Inter Vivos— Latin term that means "between the living." An inter vivos trust is created during lifetime rather than at death (testamentary). A revocable living trust is an inter vivos trust.

Irrevocable Trust— A trust that cannot be changed or canceled once it is set up. Opposite of a revocable trust.

Intestate— Dying without a will.

Joint Ownership— When two or more persons own the same asset. Can be joint tenants with rights of survivorship, tenants by the entirety or tenants in common.

Joint Tenants with Rights of Survivorship— A form of joint ownership where each owns an interest in the whole and upon death, the deceased owner's share automatically and immediately transfers to the surviving joint tenant(s).

Living Trust— A written legal document that controls, if titled in the name of your trust, your property while you are alive and well, provides for you and your loved ones in the event of disability and allows you to give what you have, to whom you want, when you want and the way you want. Ideally controls all of your assets during your lifetime and at death. Avoids probate at death and court control of assets at incapacity. Also called an inter vivos revocable trust.

Living Will— A written document declaring your intention regarding end of life issues. Generally addresses the removal of life support or life prolonging procedures in the event of a terminal illness, end stage condition or persistent vegetative state.

Peace of Mind— That sense of comfort that accompanies the knowledge that the future is secure.

Personal Representative— Another name for an executor or administrator.

Pour Over Will— A type of will often used with a living trust. It states that any assets left out of your living trust that are part of your probate estate will be "poured over" into your living trust upon your death. Requires probate.

Power of Attorney— A legal document giving legal authority to an agent who can sign your name and conduct business on your behalf in your absence. Ends at incapacity (unless it is a durable power of attorney), revocation, termination or death.

Probate— The legal process of validating a will, paying debts, and distributing assets to beneficiaries after death.

Probate Estate— The assets that go through probate after you die. Usually this includes assets you own in your individual name and those paid to your estate. Usually does not include assets owned as joint tenants with rights of survivorship, tenants by the entirety, payable-on-death or in trust for (ITF) accounts, insurance, and other assets with beneficiary designations. Assets in a trust do not go through probate.

Probate Fees— Legal, administrative, court and appraisal fees for an estate that goes through probate. Probate fees are paid from assets in the estate before the assets are fully distributed to the beneficiaries.

Revocable Trust— A trust where the creator retains the power to change, amend, revoke or cancel the trust during their lifetime. Opposite of an irrevocable trust.

Special Needs Person or Special Person— A valued member of a family that requires special consideration from an estate planning perspective because they may be unable to adequately make legal and financial decisions for themselves.

Special-Needs Trust— In the most general sense, a trust for a special person designed to preserve government assistance or to preserve a status that will allow that special person to receive government assistance in the future. May also be referred to as a supplemental needs trusts. A general term that denotes any one of several specific trusts, all of which preserve government assistance benefits.

Spendthrift Clause— Protects assets in a trust from a beneficiary's creditors. Prohibits encumbrance, alienation or the pledging of trust assets. Insulates assets from the claims of creditors.

Successor Trustee— Person or institution named in a trust that will take over the management and administration of the trust assets if the first named trustee dies, resigns, or otherwise becomes unable to act.

Supplemental Needs Trust— See Special-Needs Trust.

Testamentary Trust— A trust created in a will. Can only go into effect at death. Does not avoid probate.

Testate— One who dies with a valid will.

Testator— The individual who creates a will. Female is testatrix.

Third Party Trust— A trust established by a third party for the benefit of a special person to permit them to obtain government assistance. Created with assets that do not belong to the beneficiary or that cannot be considered to belong to the beneficiary.

Trust Corpus— The principal of a trust.

Trustee— Person or institution who manages and distributes the assets controlled by a trust according to the instructions in the trust document.

Will— (or Last Will & Testament) A written document with instructions for disposing of assets after death. Controlled by state law. A will can only be enforced through probate court.

APPENDIX B
Special People, Special Planning
Monthly Expense Worksheet
To Help You Determine How Much Money you Need

Special Person's Income
1) Government Benefits _____
2) Wages/Salary _____
3) Gifts from Family Members _____
4) Income from All Other Sources _____

   Total Income _____

Special Person's Expenses
Housing:
1) Rent _____
2) Utilities _____
       a. Electric _____
       b. Phone _____
       c. Cable _____
       d. Heating Oil _____
       e. Other _____
3) Maintenance _____
4) Cleaning Supplies _____
5) Laundry _____
6) Other Housing Expenses _____

   Total Housing Expense _____

Care Assistance:

1) Live-in Care   _____

2) Respite Care   _____

3) Custodial Care   _____

4) Other Care Assistance   _____

   Total Care Assistance Expense   _____

Personal Needs:

1) Personal Grooming   _____

   a. Hair Cuts   _____

   b. Personal Grooming Supplies   _____

2) Books, magazines, etc.   _____

3) Allowance   _____

4) Other Personal Needs   _____

   Total Personal Needs Expense   _____

Clothing   _____

Employment Costs:

1) Transportation   _____

2) Uniforms   _____

3) Training   _____

4) Meals   _____

   Total Employment Expense   _____

Education:

1) Transportation .... _____

2) Tuition/Fees .... _____

3) Books/supplies .... _____

4) Other Education Costs .... _____

Total Education Expense .... _____

Special Equipment:

1) Wheelchair .... _____

2) Elevator .... _____

3) Repair of Equipment .... _____

4) Computer .... _____

5) Audio Books .... _____

6) Ramp .... _____

7) Guide Dog .... _____

8) Technical Instruction .... _____

9) Hearing Aids/Batteries .... _____

10) Other Special Equipment .... _____

Total Special Equipment Expense ...... _____

Medical/Dental Care:

1) Doctor Visits .... _____

2) Therapy .... _____

3) Nursing Services .... _____

4) Meals for Attendants .... _____

5) Prescription Drugs, Over-The-Counter, Medicines, etc. .... _____

6) Transportation .... _____

7) Other Medical/Dental Care Costs .... _____

Total Medical/Dental Expense .... _____

Food:

1) Meals/snacks for home   _____

2) Meals/snacks away from home   _____

3) Special food requests/requirements   _____

4) Other Food Expenses   _____

   Total Food Expense   _____

Pet Care:

1) Food   _____

2) Toys   _____

3) Veterinary care   _____

4) Training   _____

5) Other Pet Expenses   _____

   Total Pet Expense   _____

Social/Recreational:

1) Sporting Events   _____

2) Special Olympics   _____

3) Spectator Sports   _____

4) Vacation Costs   _____

5) TV/VCR Rental   _____

6) Camp Costs   _____

7) Transportation   _____

8) Other Social/Recreational Expenses   _____

   Total Social/Recreational Expense   _____

Transportation Costs:

1) Automobile/Van _____

1) Gasoline _____

1) Oil, Maintenance _____

1) Other Transportation Costs _____

Total Transportation Expense _____

Miscellaneous Expenses:

1) _____

2) _____

3) _____

4) _____

Total Miscellaneous Expense _____

TOTAL EXPENSES _____

LESS: TOTAL INCOME _____

= MONTHLY SUPPLEMENTARY NEEDS _____

APPENDIX C
Special People, Special Planning
Special Letter of Instruction

_____

Prepared For: (Insert Name of Special Person)

_____

Prepared With Love By: (Insert Your Name)

_____

Date Prepared:

_____

Signature:

Personal and Family Information

Special Person:

Full Name   Date of Birth

Home Address

City   State   Zip

Phone   Fax

Email Address

Social Security #

Medical Claim #   Health Insurance Claim #

Parents:

Mother's Name   Mother's Date of Birth

Mother's Address

City   State   Zip

Mother's Phone   Fax

Mother's Email Address

Father's Name   Father's Date of Birth

Father's Address

City   State   Zip

Father's Phone   Fax

Father's Email Address

Siblings:

Name _____ Date of Birth

Address _____

City _____ State _____ Zip

Phone _____ Fax _____

Email Address _____

Relationship with Special Person _____

Name _____ Date of Birth

Address _____

City _____ State _____ Zip

Phone _____ Fax _____

Email Address _____

Relationship with Special Person _____

Name _____ Date of Birth

Address _____

City _____ State _____ Zip

Phone _____ Fax _____

Email Address _____

Relationship with Special Person _____

Siblings:

Name _____ Date of Birth _____

Address _____

City _____ State _____ Zip _____

Phone _____ Fax _____

Email Address _____

Relationship with Special Person _____

Name _____ Date of Birth _____

Address _____

City _____ State _____ Zip _____

Phone _____ Fax _____

Email Address _____

Relationship with Special Person _____

Name _____ Date of Birth _____

Address _____

City _____ State _____ Zip _____

Phone _____ Fax _____

Email Address _____

Relationship with Special Person _____

Helpers:

Guardian's Name   Guardian's Date of Birth

Guardian's Address

City   State   Zip

Guardian's Phone   Fax

Guardian's Email Address

Personal Representative's (PR) Name   PR's Date of Birth

PR's Address

City   State   Zip

PR's Phone   Fax

PR's Email Address

Trustee's Name   Trustee's Date of Birth

Trustee's Address

City   State   Zip

Trustee's Phone   Fax

Trustee's Email Address

Medical Information

Physicians:

Name
_____

Address
_____

City _____ State _____ Zip _____

Phone _____ Fax _____

Email Address
_____

Specialty/Approximate Frequency of Visits/Notes
_____

Name
_____

Address
_____

City _____ State _____ Zip _____

Phone _____ Fax _____

Email Address
_____

Specialty/Approximate Frequency of Visits/Notes
_____

Name
_____

Address
_____

City _____ State _____ Zip _____

Phone _____ Fax _____

In the Event of a Medical Emergency:

Contact Immediately: _____

_____

_____

_____

_____

_____

General Information: _____

_____

_____

_____

_____

_____

_____

Medications _____

_____

_____

_____

Allergies: _____

_____

_____

_____

Location of Medical Records: _____

_____

_____

_____

Estate Planning Information

Team Members

Attorney:

Name

Address

City   State   Zip

Phone   Fax

Email Address

Specialty/Approximate Frequency of Visits/Notes

Certified Public Accountant:

Name

Address

City   State   Zip

Phone   Fax

Email Address

Specialty/Approximate Frequency of Visits/Notes

Financial Advisor:

_____
Name

_____
Address

_____
City   State   Zip

_____
Phone   Fax

_____
Email Address

_____
Specialty/Approximate Frequency of Visits/Notes

Insurance Professional:

_____
Name

_____
Address

_____
City   State   Zip

_____
Phone   Fax

_____
Email Address

_____
Specialty/Approximate Frequency of Visits/Notes

Location of Estate Planning Documents: _____

_____

_____

_____

Estate Planning Notes and Comments: _____

_____

_____

_____

Support Contacts

Advocacy Organizations:

_____
Organization Name

_____
Person to Contact

_____
Address

_____
Phone   Fax

_____
Email Address

_____
Services Provided

_____
Organization Name

_____
Person to Contact

_____
Address

_____
Phone   Fax

_____
Email Address

_____
Organization Name

_____
Person to Contact

_____
Address

_____
Phone   Fax

_____
Email Address

_____
Services Provided

Government Assistance:

Department of Mental Health, Department of Children and Families, etc.

Organization Name

Person to Contact

Address

Phone   Fax

Email Address

Services Provided

Organization Name

Person to Contact

Address

Phone   Fax

Email Address

Services Provided

Organization Name

Person to Contact

Address

Phone   Fax

Email Address

Services Provided

Social Support:

Name

Address

City   State   Zip

Phone   Fax

Email Address

Why Important

Name

Address

City   State   Zip

Phone   Fax

Email Address

Why Important

Name

Address

City   State   Zip

Phone   Fax

Email Address

Why Important

Other important people who could provide advice and understand the principles we feel are important:

Name
_____

Address
_____

City   State   Zip
_____

Phone   Fax
_____

Email Address
_____

Explanation
_____

Name
_____

Address
_____

City   State   Zip
_____

Phone   Fax
_____

Email Address
_____

Explanation
_____

Name
_____

Address
_____

City   State   Zip
_____

Phone   Fax
_____

Email Address
_____

Explanation
_____

Educational Support:

Name

Address

City   State   Zip

Phone   Fax

Email Address

Why Important

Name

Address

City   State   Zip

Phone   Fax

Email Address

Why Important

Name

Address

City   State   Zip

Phone   Fax

Email Address

Why Important

Individuals that may be in contact but share different philosophies than we do regarding the well-being and future of our special person.

Name
_____

Address
_____

City   State   Zip
_____

Phone   Fax
_____

Email Address
_____

Why Important
_____

Name
_____

Address
_____

City   State   Zip
_____

Phone   Fax
_____

Email Address
_____

Why Important
_____

Name
_____

Address
_____

City   State   Zip
_____

Phone   Fax
_____

Email Address
_____

Why Important

Personality Traits

General description regarding what living with our special person is like

_____

_____

_____

_____

_____

_____

Basic Characteristics & Personality Traits

_____

_____

_____

_____

_____

_____

Abilities & Skills

_____

_____

_____

_____

_____

_____

Hobbies & Interests

_____

_____

_____

_____

_____

General Strengths

_____
_____
_____
_____
_____
_____

Physical Abilities:
Communication Skills

_____
_____
_____
_____
_____
_____

Physical Mobility

_____
_____
_____
_____
_____
_____

Hearing Ability

_____
_____
_____
_____
_____
_____

Seeing Ability

_____

_____

_____

_____

_____

Personal Information and Preferences:

Sizes (Clothes, Shoes, etc.)

Pants/Shorts_____ Shirt/Blouse_____ Skirt/Dress_____

Shoes_____ Coat_____ Hat_____ Gloves_____ Underwear_____

Other_____

Favorite Type of Clothes

_____

_____

_____

_____

_____

Favorite Setting/Environment (Rural/City, Large/Small Home)

_____

_____

_____

_____

Favorite Places (Places to go, people to visit, things to do)

_____

_____

_____

_____

_____

Preferred Entertainment

_____
_____
_____
_____
_____

Recreational Preferences

_____
_____
_____
_____
_____
_____

Favorite Colors and Patterns

_____
_____
_____
_____
_____
_____

Personal Habits & Hygiene:
General Comments

_____
_____
_____
_____
_____
_____
_____

How much assistance is required?

1 = Requires maximum assistance 2 = Requires some assistance

3 = Requires minimal assistance 4 = Requires no assistance

Eating_____ Shaving_____ Bathing_____

Dental Care_____ Dressing_____

Toileting_____ Personal Care_____

Communicating_____ Other_____

Food Preferences (likes and dislikes)

_____
_____
_____
_____
_____

Eating Habits

_____
_____
_____
_____
_____

Sleeping Habits

_____
_____
_____
_____
_____

Behavior (likes and dislikes)

_____

_____

_____

_____

_____

Cleanliness and Neatness

_____

_____

_____

_____

_____

General Statement of Desires

Create a vision of what you would like life to be like for your special person:

_____

_____

_____

_____

Identify the strengths that will enable your special person to reach these goals:

_____

_____

_____

_____

Identify the areas that need further development to enable your special person to achieve these goals:

_____

_____

_____

_____

_____

Identify the people you see playing major roles in helping your special person achieve these goals:

_____

_____

_____

_____

_____

APPENDIX D
Special People, Special Planning Checklist

How do we provide for our special person?

Assess:

_____ How much is currently being spent on the special person's support and maintenance?

_____ What is an estimate of these costs in future?

_____ What are the total personal assets that might be available to the special person? Carefully inventory your financial assets. Prepare a family financial statement to estimate the size of your estate currently. Then project the size of your estate into the future. What will it be in 5 years? 10 years? 20 years? Be sure to include everything you own, everything you control and everything your name is on that could potentially be used to provide for the benefit and welfare of your special person. Keep in mind the estate plan you create today, if not properly updated and maintained over time, will govern your affairs at the time of your death. Make sure it is flexible enough to meet a variety of situations, both expected and unexpected.

_____ What are the government and social programs available?

_____ How will the siblings of your special person be involved, if at all?

_____ To what degree can or will your special person be able to fend for themselves?

_____ What is the special person's prognosis for future development? It may be necessary to obtain a professional evaluation of your special person's prospects and capability to earn a living and to manage financial assets. If your special person is already an adult, you should have a fairly clear understanding of their capabilities. However, if your special person is younger, it may be more difficult to predict the future. In this case, it may be better to take a conservative view. It is far better to plan for the worst and hope for the best than to underestimate your special person's abilities or needs and not provide an adequate plan. In addition, you can always revise and update your plan as more information about your special person becomes available.

_____ Who can continue to provide for your special person's personal, legal and financial needs when original caregivers can no longer do so?

_____ Where will your special person live when no longer living with original caregivers and what is this likely to cost? Where your special person will live after your death is of paramount importance. What options are available? The type of living arrangements needed or required for your special person may drive the type of estate plan you create today. The answer to this question may depend on whether your special person will need a guardian or conservator to make decisions for them after your death. If a guardian or conservator will be required, the naming and selection of this person as set forth in your plan is critical.

_____ Can your special person work or provide any kind of gainful employment? To what extent? What are their current earnings? What is your special person's earning potential for the future? Does your special person's earnings meet all of their living expenses? or only some?

_____ Who else are the current caregivers supporting or likely to be supporting in addition to your special person? What about future caregivers?

_____ What are your feelings about taking financial resources from other children if money and resources are needed for your special person?

_____ What personal, non-governmental resources might be available to your special person (e.g., gifts from relatives, inheritances or settlements, etc.)?

_____ What federal and state government and social service programs are available now? What programs are likely to be available later? Some of the programs to consider: SSI and Medicaid for elderly, blind and disabled who also have financial need as defined by law; SSDI for a disabled adult who has sufficient employment credit toward Social Security; Social Security for Unmarried Children for a child who became disabled prior to age 22 and parent(s) also entitled to receive Social Security benefits at death, disability or retirement of parent; Medicare Part A and Part B; Medical insurance eligibility based on age and health for individuals and their dependents; state vocational rehabilitation programs; and veterans benefits.

Which planning method is best?

This answer depends on the needs of your special person, the resources available to the family and the overall needs and sophistication of other family members. It is important for the family to understand the consequences of any option it might employ to avoid unintended consequences.

Whose assets can be placed into a trust?

Generally, federal and state laws permit the assets of others to be held in trust for the benefit of a special person. These are called "third-party trusts." When a person uses their own assets, it is called a "self-settled trust."

What is the minimum amount that can be placed in trust?

Although there is no minimum fixed by law, the cost of creating and maintaining a trust might not be justified by the amount held in the trust. However, one must weigh the advantages of maintaining eligibility for benefits under Medicaid or other governmental programs against the costs of establishing and maintaining the trust plan.

How much does a trust cost?

The cost of your plan will vary depending on a number of factors including your available resources, the complexity of the plan, the expertise of the professionals involved in the plan and your commitment to keeping the plan updated over time.

Are trusts guaranteed to work?

It is impossible to have ironclad guarantees in most areas of the law, much less in this area of the law. It is more accurate to say that such trusts are designed to minimize most potential threats to the plan. The success of the trusts depends on several factors, namely the status of the laws and agencies involved with such trusts, not to mention the expertise of the professionals engaged to assist in the counseling, drafting, administration, maintenance and updating of your estate plan.

Status of the laws and agencies involved with such trusts:

Congress could change the law, or the agencies empowered to interpret those laws could make mistakes or hold contrary opinions regarding the application of the laws.

Counseling:

As with any estate plan, planning for your special person requires a thorough exploration of the family goals and resources, both human and financial.

Drafting:

There is no national standard for distributions under needs-based programs or the impact a special-needs trust distribution might have on entitlement to such programs. Each state, and even each local agency can have its own interpretation of the federal program rules. This means that a special-needs trust with poorly drafted distribution standards could make your special person ineligible for program benefits or could prevent your special person from enjoying many services that might be available under a properly drafted plan. Either alternative may defeat the family's goals and objectives.

It is advisable to provide training and written instructions to the trustees outlining their duties, the rules governing distributions on behalf of your special person and reporting standards. Special letters of instruction will be invaluable guides for current and future caregivers in the implementation of the plan for your special person.

Special trust provisions like "poison pills" anticipate circumstances that could result in the provisions of the special-needs trust being ineffective or invalid and therefore cause your special person to be ineligible for future benefits. The poison pill might direct that trust assets will be held for your special person by alternate beneficiaries such as siblings, allowing your special person to maintain eligibility for benefits.

At the death of a special person, state law differs regarding what happens to the balance of special-needs trust assets when the special person is gone or the special-needs trust is found to be invalid. Drafting must set forth how the balance of the trust assets are to be distributed to protect them from the claims of state or federal agencies.

Administration:
Even a properly drafted trust can't maintain a person's eligibility for benefits if the trustee makes distributions that are inconsistent with the family's plan for the special person. An improper distribution could cause the disabled person to become ineligible for benefits. On the other hand, there are times when disqualifying distributions are in the best interests of the special person. Trustees must be able to understand entitlement strategies that will enhance your special person's quality of life, while maximizing available resources.

Maintenance and Updating:

The plan for your special person is not a one-time event, it is a process that lasts a lifetime. The proper implementation of your plan requires careful, consistent and structured maintenance and updating. Change is continuous—in our personal lives, in the law (state and federal) and in the way your attorney practices law. Seek out practitioners and processes that employ a systematic means for ensuring the success of your estate plan.

About The Authors

PEGGY R. HOYT, J.D., M.B.A.

Peggy is the oldest of four daughters born to John A. Hoyt and Gertrude M. "Trudy" Hoyt. She was born in Dearborn, Michigan, and spent her first 10 years as a "PK," or "preacher's kid," before her father joined The Humane Society of the United States in 1970. Peggy graduated with an A.A. degree from Marymount University in Arlington, Virginia; earned a B.B.A. and M.B.A. from Stetson University in DeLand, Florida; and earned a J.D. from Stetson University College of Law in St. Petersburg, Florida.

Peggy has worked in a number of fields including college recruiting at Embry-Riddle Aeronautical University and financial consulting at Merrill Lynch. She also served as chief financial officer for Fine Foliage of Florida, Inc.

Today, Peggy and her law partner, Randy Bryan, own and operate Hoyt & Bryan, LLC. Her law firm limits its practice to estate planning and administration, including special-needs planning, pet planning, elder law and guardianships. She also works in the areas of business creation and succession as well as real estate and corporate transactions.

Peggy is the author of a one-of-a kind book called *All My Children Wear Fur Coats – How to Leave a Legacy for Your Pet* available through her law office, your favorite bookstore or by visiting www.legacyforyourpet.com.

She is active in a variety of organizations, including the National Network of Estate Planning Attorneys, as a regular speaker on estate planning topics and contributor of practice management materials. In addition, she serves as co-chair of the Orange County Bar Association Solo and Small Firm Committee, as trustee to Stetson University's Business School Foundation, and as a board member of The Harmony Institute, a not-for-profit organization. Peggy speaks regularly to the Center for Autism and Related Disorders, a program of the University of Central Florida.

Peggy's passion is her pets, so when she is not working on building her law practice, writing or speaking, she is spending time "playing" with her wild mustang horses; Reno and Tahoe, and her Premarin rescue, Sierra; her dogs, Kira, Corkie and Tiger; and her cats, Beijing, Bangle, Cuddles and Tommy.

CANDACE M. POLLOCK, J.D.

Prior to attending law school, Candace owned a business that provided claim review and consulting services to Ohio lawyers in the area of workers' compensation and Social Security claims—areas involving the rights of disabled people. During this period she was a founding member and first acting president of the Women Business Owner's Association (now known as the Cleveland Chapter of the National Association of Women Business Owners).

Candace was encouraged to attend law school by her attorney-clients and graduated from Cleveland-Marshall College of Law in 1986. After graduation, she joined Hahn & Swadey—a firm established in 1951—and later became partner, forming Hahn, Swadey & Pollock. Finally, upon the retirement of Robert Swadey, the firm became Hahn & Pollock.

Candace continued representing disabled people while expanding her practice to include estate and financial planning, probate and elder law services in response to the needs of her clients.

Her participation in professional and community activities has been "eclectic" and runs the gamut from board member of a neighborhood association to president of a local non-profit athletic (rowing) organization. She has held various leadership roles in legal and professional associations, including: chair of the Workers' Compensation and Social Security Section of the Cuyahoga County Bar Association, Representative-at-Large on the Board of Trustees of the Ohio Academy of Trial Lawyers (OATL) and executive committee member of the Workers' Compensation Section of OATL. She participates in non-board positions in other non-profit, charitable and political organizations.

She is currently a mentor coach in the Practice Builder Program of the National Network of Estate Planning Attorneys (NNEPA). In this national program, she helps coach attorneys in effective business management and marketing practices to help them create practices that meet the needs of their clients and families.

In addition, she teaches individuals and organizations about various disability and estate planning topics.

Contact Us:

Peggy and Candace are available as speakers and for interviews and
are happy to contribute written material to publications regarding planning
for special people. Please feel free to contact them at:

Hoyt & Bryan, LLC
251 Plaza Drive, Suite B
Oviedo, Florida 32765
(407) 977-8080 (T)
(407) 977-8078 (F)
peggy@hoytbryan.com
www.hoytbryan.com

Hahn & Pollock
820 West Superior Avenue, Suite 510
Cleveland, Ohio 44113
(216) 861-6160 (T)
(216) 861-5272 (F)
info@HAHNPOLLOCK.com
www.HAHNPOLLOCK.com

or visit their web site designed especially for you and your special person,
www.specialpeoplespecialplanning.com.

Printed in the United States
25086LVS00004B/100-141